Advance Acclaim for
Chasing the High

"*Chasing the High* is an excellent resource on substance abuse for adolescents and their families. Keegan's personal story captures the experience of addiction and recovery in a compelling manner. The authors even make the neurobiology of addiction clear and accessible. It is difficult to find good resources about addictive drugs for adolescents and this book fills the gap."

—Charles Dackis, M.D.,
Director, Charles O'Brien Center for Addiction Treatment,
University of Pennsylvania

"*Chasing the High* is honest and intense, yet also extremely informative. Kyle Keegan has written a brave cautionary tale that takes his readers deep inside the belly of addiction. This book speaks to anyone who has ever felt the deadly grip of drugs and alcohol take hold, but also to those who have watched someone they love disappear into a dark cloud of chemicals. Bravo to Kyle for having the courage to share his painful and inspiring story with the world."

—Lynn Marie Smith, author of Rolling Away: My Agony with Ecstasy

"While the perils of addiction are often lost in detailed data, there remains a lacuna of information on the personal tolls of substance abuse. In *Chasing the High* we are given an intriguing and very personal snapshot of the initiation, maintenance, and subsequent battling of severe chemical dependency—intermixed with factual and useful information about addictions. Along with the author, we experience the tribulations of the addiction—from the crashes to the euphoria to the rehabilitation and optimism of experiencing life without drugs. *Chasing the High* provides a unique inside perspective on addiction that is often lost in academic texts."

—Timothy E. Wilens, M.D.,
Massachusetts General Hospital & Harvard Medical School

"*Chasing the High* by Keegan and Moss is a wonderful first-hand account of a young person's development of addiction. With powerful descriptions of the events that led to drug use, abuse, and addiction the authors succeed in weaving a primer on addiction within the developing saga. Engaging and easy to read, this book should be an enormous help for those individuals and families struggling with this disorder to understand addiction. Particularly poignant for this researcher is the repeated focus on the 'dark side' of addiction. The author states, 'In fact, you're taking drugs now not so much to feel good as to keep from feeling bad.' The authors illustrate so clearly that seeking drugs to fill emotional holes creates even bigger emotional holes that in turn need to be filled. This phenomenon is the core feature of addiction."

—George F. Koob, Ph.D.,
Professor, Committee on the Neurobiology of Addictive Disorders,
The Scripps Research Institute

The Annenberg Foundation Trust at Sunnylands'
Adolescent Mental Health Initiative

Patrick E. Jamieson, Ph.D., *series editor*

Other books in the series

For young people

Mind Race: A Firsthand Account of One Teenager's Experience With Bipolar Disorder
Patrick E. Jamieson, Ph.D., with Moira A. Rynn, M.D.

Monochrome Days: A Firsthand Account of One Teenager's Experience With Depression
Cait Irwin, with Dwight L. Evans, M.D., and Linda Wasmer Andrews

*What You Must Think of Me: A Firsthand Account of One Teenager's Experience With
Social Anxiety Disorder*
Emily Ford, with Michael Liebowitz, M.D., and Linda Wasmer Andrews

*Next to Nothing: A Firsthand Account of One Teenager's Experience With
an Eating Disorder*
Carrie Arnold, with B. Timothy Walsh, M.D.

*Me, Myself, and Them: A Firsthand Account of One Young Person's Experience
With Schizophrenia*
Kurt Snyder, with Raquel E. Gur, M.D., and Linda Wasmer Andrews

*The Thought That Counts: A Firsthand Account of One Teenager's Experience
With Obsessive-Compulsive Disorder*
Jared Douglas Kant, with Martin Franklin, Ph.D., and Linda Wasmer Andrews

Eight Stories Up: An Adolescent Chooses Hope Over Suicide
DeQuincy A. Lezine, Ph.D., with David Brent, M.D. (forthcoming, 2008)

For parents and other adults

If Your Adolescent Has Depression or Bipolar Disorder
Dwight L. Evans, M.D., and Linda Wasmer Andrews

If Your Adolescent Has an Eating Disorder
B. Timothy Walsh, M.D., and V. L. Cameron

If Your Adolescent Has an Anxiety Disorder
Edna B. Foa, Ph.D., and Linda Wasmer Andrews

If Your Adolescent Has Schizophrenia
Raquel E. Gur, M.D., Ph.D., and Ann Braden Johnson, Ph.D.

Chasing the High

*A Firsthand Account of One
Young Person's Experience
With Substance Abuse*

Kyle Keegan

with Howard B. Moss, M.D.

The Annenberg Foundation Trust at Sunnylands'
Adolescent Mental Health Initiative

2008

OXFORD
UNIVERSITY PRESS

Oxford University Press, Inc., publishes works that further
Oxford University's objective of excellence
in research, scholarship, and education.

The Annenberg Foundation Trust at Sunnylands
The Annenberg Public Policy Center of the University of Pennsylvania
Oxford University Press

Oxford   New York
Auckland   Cape Town   Dar es Salaam   Hong Kong   Karachi
Kuala Lumpur   Madrid   Melbourne   Mexico City   Nairobi
New Delhi   Shanghai   Taipei   Toronto

With offices in
Argentina   Austria   Brazil   Chile   Czech Republic   France   Greece
Guatemala   Hungary   Italy   Japan   Poland   Portugal   Singapore
South Korea   Switzerland   Thailand   Turkey   Ukraine   Vietnam

Published by Oxford University Press, Inc.
198 Madison Avenue, New York, New York 10016

www.oup.com

Oxford is a registered trademark of Oxford University Press

Library of Congress Cataloging-in-Publication Data
Keegan, Kyle, 1975-
Chasing the high : a firsthand account of one young person's experience
with substance abuse / by Kyle Keegan, with Howard B. Moss.
p. cm. — (Adolescent mental health initiative)
Includes bibliographical references and index.
ISBN-13: 978-0-19-531471-7 (cloth)
ISBN-13: 978-0-19-531472-4 (pbk)
1. Keegan, Kyle, 1975-   2. Substance abuse–United States—Biography.
3. Recovering addicts—United States—Biography.   I. Moss, Howard.   II. Title.
HV5805.K42A3 2008
616.86092—dc22   2007035423

9 8 7 6 5 4 3 2 1
Printed in the United States of America
on acid-free paper

Contents

Foreword   ix

Preface   xiii

The History Behind Chasing the High   xiv

What to Expect From This Book   xv

One
Crash and Rescue   3

Above the City, Steeped in Misery   4

Back From the Edge   7

Substance Abuse and Addiction Defined   8

Addiction Is a Disease   11

A Hellish Journey   12

Two
The Early Days of Using   15

My Not-So-Shady Past   15

A Forbidden Sip   17

One Puff Leads to Another   20

My Uncertain Future   23

Heroin   25

A Rite of Passage Versus the Slippery Slope to Addiction   27

The Ride Down That Slope 30
Who Becomes Addicted, Who Does Not, and Why? 33

Three
The Noose Tightens 46
A Moment of Truth, and Then Denial 46
First Shot at Detoxification 49
Learning the Life of an Addict 51
Desperate Moves 53
Returning to an Unfamiliar Home 56
"This Is Your Brain on Drugs" 59
Different Types of Drugs of Abuse 73

Four
Trying to Get Help 91
Overconfidence and Denial: Do Not Mix 92
A Minor Arrest 94
A Major Arrest 96
Up, Down, Up, Down—The Saga of Addiction Continues 98
A Crucial Turning Point 99
Substance Abuse Treatment: What to Expect 101
Treatment of Co-occurring Mental Disorders 118

Five
Recovery 122
What Does Recovery Mean for You? 124
If a Relapse Occurs . . . 136

Six
Looking Back, Looking Ahead 138
"Real" Recovery Is Whatever Works for Us 139

Frequently Asked Questions 141
Glossary 149

Resources   153

Bibliography   159

Index   161

Foreword

The Adolescent Mental Health Initiative (AMHI) was created by The Annenberg Foundation Trust at Sunnylands to share with mental health professionals, parents, and adolescents the advances in treatment and prevention now available to adolescents with mental health disorders. The Initiative was made possible by the generosity and vision of Ambassadors Walter and Leonore Annenberg, and the project was administered through the Annenberg Public Policy Center of the University of Pennsylvania in partnership with Oxford University Press.

The Initiative began in 2003 with the convening, in Philadelphia and New York, of seven scholarly commissions made up of over 150 leading psychiatrists and psychologists from around the country. Chaired by Drs. Edna B. Foa, Dwight L. Evans, B. Timothy Walsh, Martin E. P. Seligman, Raquel E. Gur, Charles P. O'Brien, and Herbert Hendin, these commissions were tasked with assessing the state of scientific research on the prevalent mental disorders whose onset occurs predominantly between the ages of 10 and 22. Their collective findings now appear in a book for mental health professionals and policy makers titled *Treating and Preventing Adolescent Mental Health Disorders* (2005). As the first product of the Initiative, that book also identified a research agenda that would best advance our ability to prevent and treat these disorders, among them anxiety disorders, depression and bi-polar disorder, eating disorders, substance abuse, and schizo-phrenia.

The second prong of the Initiative's three-part effort is a series of smaller books for general readers. Some of the books are designed primarily for parents of adolescents with a specific mental health disorder. And some, including this one, are aimed at adolescents themselves who are struggling with a mental illness. All of the books draw their scientific informa-tion in part from the AMHI professional volume, presenting it in a manner that is accessible to general readers of different ages. The "teen books" also feature the real-life story of one young person who has struggled with—and now manages—a given mental illness. They serve as both a source of solid research about the illness and as a roadmap to recovery for afflicted young people. Thus they offer a unique combina-tion of medical science and firsthand practical wisdom in an effort to inspire adolescents to take an active role in their own recovery.

The third part of the Sunnylands' Adolescent Mental Health Initiative consists of two Web sites. The first, www. CopeCareDeal.org, addresses teens. The second, www.oup. com/us/teenmentalhealth, provides updates to the medical community on matters discussed in *Treating and Preventing Adolescent Mental Health Disorders,* the AMHI professional book.

We hope that you find this volume, as one of the fruits of the Initiative, to be helpful and enlightening.

Patrick Jamieson, Ph.D.
Series Editor
Adolescent Risk Communication Institute
Annenberg Public Policy Center
University of Pennsylvania
Philadelphia, PA

Preface

Working on this book has not been easy. I've had to plunge deep into the memories of my years of addiction, and into the troubling emotions that I felt back then. If you're reading this book right now, chances are you already have some notion of the uncomfortable feelings that substance abuse can cause. I believe that this book can be helpful to you and to others who have faced the incredible challenge of addiction, so I've traveled back in time in order to relate to you my experiences with drugs—mostly heroin—and how I nearly lost my life to this devastating substance.

I started using alcohol and drugs in high school, and the sensations that they produced quickly carried me off to a place where I didn't care about my friends, family, or my own future. I was soon living as a homeless junkie in California, far away from the place where I'd grown up and from those who cared about me. I was so in thrall to heroin that nothing else mattered; my life became so bad that I eventually began to contemplate suicide. I was miserable and couldn't see any way out of the desperate situation I'd gotten myself into; death seemed to be the only solution.

As you can see, I was wrong about that. Today I'm clean, and it's been two years since I've been dependent on heroin. I have an exciting and unusual job as a commercial diver, a family that loves and supports me, and a happy wife and baby. I have hobbies and interests that don't involve drugs or alcohol. Finally, in my early thirties, with a lot of hard work and the appropriate treatment, I've been able to turn my life around, and I have no intention of going back.

If you gain nothing else from reading this book, know this: you *can* overcome an addiction. You may be having a difficult time, struggling with whether or not you have a substance abuse problem—or you may already know that you're in trouble. If you're willing to recognize that you need help, and accept help when it appears, then you have every chance of returning from the brink and reclaiming your life. As you'll see, I was just about as close to losing my life to drugs as anyone ever can be, and I made it back. You can too. My modest hope is that this book, and the experiences and information it contains, can help you on your road to recovery.

The History Behind *Chasing the High*

The idea for this book was born in 2003, when seven scholarly commissions on adolescent mental health were convened by the Annenberg Foundation Trust at Sunnylands. The psychiatrists and psychologists on these commissions were charged with examining the state of the science on mental disorders that strike teenagers and young adults. Several books on, or drawing from, the findings of these commissions followed, including the one you hold in your hands.

Howard B. Moss, M.D., was a member of the commission on substance use disorders, and he is also the medical adviser for this book. Dr. Moss is an addiction psychiatrist and a professor of clinical psychiatry at the George Washington University School of Medicine. He also holds a post at the National Institute of Alcohol Abuse and Alcoholism, so he brings a wealth of experience and wisdom to these pages.

What to Expect From This Book

Dr. Moss and I have joined forces to create a book that is different from others on substance abuse in young people. Some books tell one person's story of addiction, but offer little in the way of straightforward, reliable information on getting treatment and staying in recovery. Others focus on treatment and recovery alone, offering no personal perspective of what it's really like to deal with drug abuse. This book, on the other hand, looks at substance abuse from both points of view. Intended primarily for young people, *Chasing the High* is my own firsthand account of addiction as well as a useful, easy-to-understand resource on substance abuse, treatment, and recovery. Each chapter is divided into two halves: The first describes my personal struggle with drugs, while the second looks at the science, medicine, and social trends of substance abuse, which affected not only me but other young people as well. In addition, because no two people experience substance abuse and drug addiction in exactly the same way, I thought it would be useful to give some different perspectives on the issue, so I have included the voices of other recovering addicts alongside my own story.

Before we get started, I should mention that although I discuss certain treatment options and medications, I don't mean to recommend that you adopt any of the therapies that my care providers and I developed for me. The best course of treatment for you should be determined in collaboration with your own qualified doctors and therapists. Also, I want to offer the admission that the events I'm about to describe occurred over the course of many years, and during a lot of that time I wasn't exactly in my right mind. I've tried to relate my experiences as accurately and completely as possible, and any omissions or errors I may have made during this narrative are entirely unintentional.

I invite you to join me as I recount the often-harrowing experiences that cost me nearly ten years of my life. You may be feeling hopeless or helpless in the face of your drug use, and confused as to how to proceed and what to expect. I'm here to tell you that recovery is possible—probable, even—if you give it your all. I hope that I might be able to offer some guidance and help direct you toward a brighter future, where drugs don't control us or dictate the decisions we make.

Chasing the High

Chapter One

Crash and Rescue

---

ooking back on those years I spent barely surviving on the
streets as a heroin addict, it's hard to believe that I'm here
now to tell you my story. But I want you to know what it was
like, and what a drug addiction really means.

I'm going to start not at the beginning, but in a place that
stands out in my mind above all others in the haze of my drug-
using days: Long Beach, California. My experiences there rep-
resent my addiction at its very worst. Next I'll tell you how I
ended up there, the son of a loving, hard-working, middle-class
family, born and raised in a small town in New York State.
Finally, I'll show you how I was able—with a lot of help—to
find my way back to a decent and healthy life. Along the way,
I'll also be giving you an idea of what science knows about
addiction in young people—like
why teenagers are at higher risk
for abusing drugs, and how even
a ruthless addiction like mine
can be overcome. When people,
especially kids, start using drugs,
they often don't understand how

*I'm going to level with you
throughout this book, and
the real truth about the
worst seems like the best
place to start.*

dangerous this experimentation can be—even if they've been using for a while with no serious repercussions. But I'm going to level with you throughout this book, and the real truth about the worst seems like the best place to start.

So, back to Long Beach. I ended up there because I'd stolen some cash and drugs while I was living in Arizona. My friends (other addicts I was hanging out with at the time) and I came to the conclusion that we'd better relocate. After acquiring a stolen truck, we headed west to California.

The weeks we spent in Long Beach flew by, but our daily schedule didn't change much; the routine was getting high and stealing what we needed to survive. Friends and I would meet in front of a laundromat every morning to purchase wake-up shots of heroin. The supply of the drug we planned to save until morning somehow never made it through the night.

Above the City, Steeped in Misery

I'd been sleeping on a rooftop for several weeks now. I felt there was some kind of security in sleeping above everything. Not that I was safe, of course—it was just as easy to get robbed on a rooftop as it was in an alley, where I also spent many nights. I had a setup on that roof of a few milk crates, an old couch frame, and two cushions that smelled horribly of urine from the prior inhabitants. I kept a small garbage bag containing my possessions nearby. When you're homeless, the less you have, the less you have to worry about getting stolen or lugging around with you.

Unlike in New York, where drugs had been available at any hour, in Long Beach heroin had to be bought on a schedule: once at night and once in the morning. On this particular night, as I was finishing up a round of shoplifting from some convenience stores in the Korean section of Long Beach, I noticed that I was running a little behind schedule. I quickly made my way to a fence who bought stolen goods, getting enough money to then go and try to secure a relaxing evening of speedballs—heroin mixed with cocaine—on my favorite rooftop. Unfortunately, I was too late. As I rounded the corner, I watched in horror as my fellow junkies scurried off and the dealer's car sped away.

My first instinct was to catch up with slowest of the receding bunch and ask if I could purchase something to hold me through the night, since the next delivery wouldn't be until morning. Instead of getting the fix I had hoped for, I was offered a matchhead of cocaine. Against my better judgment, I accepted it and made my way to my roof. You see, though I knew that cocaine without heroin would only make me feel sicker, I was an addict, and therefore unable to turn down any drug. Once back on my couch overlooking West Long Beach, I quickly fixed up the shot of cocaine.

After about fifteen seconds, the cocaine euphoria began wearing off. This was the part I hated most, and the regrets started to roll in. My mind raced and I panicked. How was I going to make it until morning with no more drugs, when it was barely 8:00 P.M.?

For a moment I thought about my life up until then. My drug addiction had left a trail of destruction in my wake—I'd robbed, stolen, cheated, lied. My family had long since disowned me. I felt more and more overwhelmingly that my days were numbered, and at the rate I was going, something had to give soon.

Back on my rooftop, I started feeling something that I would have given anything to avoid. The cocaine had worn off and a sickness was quickly spreading through me. That was bad enough, but when I began to shake violently and to feel as if my body temperature were dropping rapidly, I knew that I had what we called "cotton fever," an extremely unpleasant physical reaction to the drug I'd just taken.

Caused by a bacterium that infects certain cotton plants and is then injected accidentally through a cotton filter and into the body, cotton fever was maybe one of the worst feelings imaginable. For the hour or two that it lasted I could look forward to every muscle and nerve in my body tensing up to the point of excruciating pain, along with extreme cold and uncontrollable tremors. Add that to the crash I was experiencing from the cocaine, and the heroin sickness from not getting my nightly fix, and I was in for an evening of great misery and despair. And just when I thought that I had finally reached the lowest possible level of physical and emotional agony, I realized it could get worse . . . I felt the first drop of rain.

I drifted in and out of consciousness for most of the night, not sure where nightmares left off and reality picked up. Several times I hallucinated, thinking someone was calling me from the courtyard down below. I would find myself teetering on a ledge two stories up, yelling into the darkness of the cold rain. If I'd had the nerve I would have just hurled myself off the edge and put an end to this insanity. But the insanity was far from over. Somehow I made it through that awful night and scored my wake-up heroin the next morning. I was at it all over again.

You can't possibly know how bad addiction feels unless you've been there. You can read a hundred books, see a thousand movies, even work with addicts every day as a counselor or therapist. You still know nothing about the nature of the beast, the power, the emptiness, the broken heart, the numb mind. That voice that forever speaks in your head. That voice that pushes you, that beats you, that empties you—that voice that, in the end, is your own.

Back From the Edge

Today the voice in my head tells me something different.

I've heard people refer to a high as something like what it must feel like to be in the womb. My feeling is that getting clean is like being born. It's like being thrust into an alien world—sharp, bright, and cold. The senses come alive again. It's painful, beautiful, and scary all at once. As great as the feeling of getting high can seem, I now know that it is no comparison to waking up early and watching the sun come up on a summer morning, knowing that I do not need to stick a needle in my arm today.

> Getting clean is like being born.... It's painful, beautiful, and scary all at once.

How did I get from that rooftop in Long Beach to where I am today, reconciled with my family, happily married with a beautiful child, working at an exciting career doing something that I love? The famous philosopher Søren Kierkegaard tells part of the story. "A man may accomplish many feats and comprehend a vast amount of knowledge, and still have no understanding of himself," he wrote, "yet suffering directs us to look inward; if it succeeds, then there, within us, is the beginning of our learning." I had to learn about myself, to look deeper into myself than I could ever imagine, in order to get free of drugs.

For much of my life before I started to use drugs, I felt out of place. No matter how hard I tried to be smart, and to be the best at everything I did, I couldn't shake the feeling that I somehow just didn't belong. I could not stand to be myself and eventually learned to escape these bad feelings by altering my state of mind with foreign substances. I endured many years of life as a drug addict before I thought to look inside myself for real explanations for my emotional discomfort.

My suffering—and the suffering I'd caused my loved ones—compelled me to look deep inside, right down to my core, in order to understand why I punished myself and those around me. I soon realized that I had never truly accepted myself for who I was. In time, I developed a relationship with myself and figured out that the more my self-esteem grew and the more I learned to love myself, the less need I would have for the drugs I had used to mask my feelings, emotions, and even my identity.

I remember sitting in an abandoned car in an empty lot once, pushing a shot off into my arm, looking up at the person next to me, and saying, "This is it, this is all I will ever be." Thankfully, I was mistaken. Today I can honestly say that, for the first time in many years, I am happy. In the last couple of years, the destruction I've caused has actually begun to mend. My family is no longer ashamed of me, and, importantly, I am no longer ashamed of myself. I am a responsible, caring, productive person—someone I never thought I would be.

My trip to hell and back may sound familiar to you, or it may seem hideously foreign. I'm not the only one who has taken it, though, and as you'll see, there is real science behind my struggles. There are researchers who have devoted their careers to studying why people like me end up addicted to drugs—why we choose to take that first sip of alcohol at a too-young age, why we go on to try harder and more dangerous drugs and become hooked on them, and how we're finally able to turn our lives around—or, tragically, why we're sometimes not able to. I think that knowing why we do the things we do is a key part of changing our own destructive behavior.

Substance Abuse and Addiction Defined

It's important to note that there is a difference between substance *abuse* and substance *dependence*. The term *substance abuse* with regard to adolescents is defined in medical circles as the use of alcohol and/or illegal drugs despite the occurrence of negative consequences; *substance dependence,* on the other hand, is much more serious and is associated with a loss of control of drug taking, mental and behavioral disturbances, and some harmful physical symptoms. Substance abuse can easily escalate and become dependence. Doctors and therapists often use the term *addiction* interchangeably with dependence, and you will find that I tend to use that term myself when describing my own experiences with drugs.

Even people who abuse drugs or alcohol but are fortunate enough to escape the pain and degradation of addiction will find that their lives can be adversely affected by their use. If you use drugs or alcohol, you may find your physical and mental health deteriorating. Your schoolwork may suffer, as might your job or extracurricular activities, such as sports. Your relationships might become strained and difficult, and you may find yourself in trouble with the law. My point here is that drug and alcohol use can have a surprisingly harmful effect on the quality of your life even if you do not develop a full-blown addiction like I did. Car accidents, lost jobs, poor grades, unhappy relationships, arrests, and physical injuries are only some of the negative consequences of drug and alcohol use.

Sliding Into the Mire

Seventeen-year-old Matthew (a pseudonym) wrote that for him none of life's hardships was as difficult as getting out of the drug world. Here he describes his escalating drug use and the denial that allowed him to continue:

(continued)

I did not think I had a problem. I was starting defensive back on the freshman football team, I was keeping my grades up, and I was dating a junior. Besides, my parents did not have a clue. I felt like everything was going my way. What I did not realize, at the time, was that for every action there is a consequence, and my actions were building up consequences I could not have foreseen.

I first realized I had a problem when my girlfriend dumped me. I thought I didn't care, and I told myself I just used her like she used me. I did not shed a tear. I did, however, increase the amount of drugs flowing into my body. One of my favorite combinations was alcohol and marijuana. I felt like I was doing somersaults and forgetting all my problems at the same time—what a deal! I later learned from my father, who is a doctor, that I could have died very easily from alcohol poisoning this way. . . .

So began my downward slide into the mire. As my black hole of need grew larger, I filled it with more and more. LSD, cocaine, crack, pills, and inhalants all became a part of my life. I started dealing drugs to support my habit. To me, marijuana was no longer something to look forward to. It was something I used morning, noon, and night just to feel "normal." (Reprinted from *Teens Write Through It: Essays from Teens Who Have Triumphed Over Trouble* [New York: Fairview Press, 1998].)

With habitual use, drugs begin to trigger the changes in brain chemistry that lead to addiction. If you use drugs, you might have found, for example, that lately you need bigger and bigger doses to get the same effects—that "high" or "rush"— that you once experienced with a much smaller dose. Your brain has begun to develop what scientists call *tolerance* to the substance. You are now almost certainly psychologically dependent on the drug—meaning you have begun to use the drug to improve the way you feel emotionally, to lighten your mood, or to relax you. This increase in dosage will almost inevitably lead you into riskier and riskier situations, resulting in bad decisions, psychological symptoms like paranoia and/or depression, and physical symptoms like damage to the lungs, liver, and brain.

By this time you're what the scientists call physically dependent on the drug, and using it is not a choice but a compulsion. You must use the drug to avoid the physical effects of *withdrawal*—a set of symptoms that occurs when habitual drug use ends suddenly—and you feel really bad when you do not take it for an extended period. In fact, you're taking drugs now not so much to feel good as to keep from feeling bad. An addicted person may ruminate or obsess about using drugs, and cravings invade your life, blotting out everything else that used to be important to you. The changes in the brain may now be permanent. Now, simply wanting to stop—in fact all the willpower in the world—cannot alone help you to overcome the addiction. Only professional addiction treatment, along with enormous effort on your part, can pull you back toward a healthy, normal life.

Addiction Is a Disease

The consensus among researchers and doctors today is that addiction is a disease. And in fact, many of the behaviors and symptoms of drug addiction resemble those seen in medical illnesses, such as tangible differences in the brains of those with addictions when compared to individuals with no addiction, the tendency of addictions to be hereditary, and the risk of relapse. Unfortunately, the general public still views drug addiction as a matter solely of independent choice and personal morality. Drug addicts such as myself are deemed unrepentant criminals instead of sufferers of a serious brain disease; this is why so many drug addicts wind up in jail instead of in treatment. While it is true that I decided of my own will to use heroin for the first time—and, for that matter, to take my first sip of alcohol, and to take that first drag of marijuana—it didn't take long for the drug to hijack my brain and wrest away control over my life.

Years ago, First Lady Nancy Reagan led an antidrug campaign based on the idea that kids should "just say no" to drugs. In fact, people used to say that to me all the time. What they didn't understand was that, once I was fully in the grip of my addiction, I was incapable of "saying no." Deciding I had to stop taking heroin was the first step, and I did have to make that decision on my own. But actually overcoming my addiction was far beyond my power to accomplish all by myself. It was a long process that would have been impossible without a lot of support and treatment from trained professionals. I needed to look for strength inside myself, but I also needed the continuing and skillful support and help of others.

A Hellish Journey

As you follow me on my journey through hell and back, you will see that the disease of addiction happens on two very different levels—as I experienced it, and as the scientists say it affected my brain and body. You'll see that my addiction involved both my cells and my spirit, both my brain and my mind.

My tale traces a pretty typical course followed by people who develop an addiction, whether it be to alcohol, cocaine, methamphetamine, heroin, or some other drug. Like me, they saw their chances of living normal, satisfying lives threatened, and in many cases obliterated by dependence on one or more chemicals that can seriously damage the human brain. My experience with drugs began with experimentation, but I soon became increasingly fascinated and then infatuated with the sensations they produced. Finally, I became unable to function without drugs, and moved on to compulsive, irresistible use that was totally out of my control. This cost me my relationships with my family and my true friends, countless jobs, my self-respect, and my ties to regular society. It almost cost me my sanity and even my life.

But, in other ways, my story is also pretty rare. That's because only a minority of the many young people who start messing around with harmful substances ultimately develop the chronic brain disease of addiction. Scientific research has shown us that certain people are at higher risk than average for undergoing the changes in the brain that transform "social" drug use and experimentation into the kind of addiction that takes over and wrecks lives. I was one of those people, but of course I didn't know that at the beginning.

And so, since most people won't ever abuse drugs on the extreme level that I did, my experience will serve as a cautionary tale, a series of mistakes to be avoided at all costs. However, for the people who are like me, who have sunk into the dismal depths of true addiction, I hope that my story will serve as a lifeline, a compass to help navigate the treacherous course back to a healthy, drug-free existence. For me, it was a long and difficult road, and there were a lot of attempts, setbacks, and failures before I managed to accomplish the goal of getting into recovery and staying there. Now that I have succeeded at this huge task, I have made maintaining my recovery the top priority in my daily life. It gets my continuing effort and attention.

... I have made maintaining my recovery the top priority in my daily life.

Make no mistake: recovery is not easy. It is not foolproof, and it is not fun. It can't make up for the time lost and opportunities missed out on while you were using. It *can* give you a second chance at a normal life. Let me repeat what that chance has given me: Overcoming my addiction allowed me to repair my relationships with my parents, and to find true love with my wife and our new family. I've been able to develop my ability for writing and have embarked upon an exciting career. I've even been back to school—this time it was a pleasure—to get the training I needed to dive as a pro. I know that if I can do all this, then you can, too. With the proper treatment and a healthy dose of hard work, you can walk the hard path from the pain of addiction to the rewards of recovery. I hope you'll let me be one of your guides on that trip, and that this book will help you find your way.

Chapter Two

The Early Days of Using

I t may or may not surprise you to learn that I can't say exactly why I started using drugs in the first place. I don't have a simple explanation, nor any that will completely satisfy you— or, for that matter, satisfy even me. I can only say that I had certain uncomfortable and unpleasant emotional feelings during my childhood and adolescence, and I found that using various substances helped me feel better. This was obviously a poor solution to my troubles, and caused me and my family problems that were infinitely more serious. I simply lacked the insight and maturity to see that back then.

But a lot of kids lack maturity, and some of them make bad choices as a result. Perhaps seeing the terrible consequences of some of my worst decisions will help you to make wiser choices in your own life.

My Not-So-Shady Past

From what you've read so far about my past, you may have guessed that I don't come from an abusive family in a violent urban slum—the scenario that many people assume lurks in an addict's background. No, mine was a close, caring, and even overprotective middle-class family in a small town. I was born to unconditionally loving parents who would eventually prove to be the strongest people I have ever known.

I grew up on a nice street in Upstate New York where the houses stand on less than five acres each, in a neighborhood surrounded by some nearby woods. My dad had a career with the Forestry Department and had worked his way up to a supervisor's position. It was his job to maintain the two thousand acres of forested land in our county and in the next one over. He loved the outdoors and passed that love on to me. In addition to various part-time jobs, my mom's main occupation was taking care of us and the house—considered by some to be a full-time job in and of itself.

Growing up, I had a vast and vivid imagination. I spent a lot of time exploring the woods around the house. The kids who lived on our street usually played together, but I enjoyed most the times when it was just me, alone in the forest constructing imaginary worlds of mystery and magic. I was full of life, light, and love, so full of innocence. My father and I would often go hiking, fishing, and camping. We were the epitome of a loving father and son. I was close with my mother, too.

But at some point in my childhood I began to feel great pressure to fit in with the other kids, pressure to be cool, to be accepted by others. These feelings opened a gap that would slowly distance me from my family. By the time I was around eight or nine years old I began to think I was not as strong or as fast or even as smart as most of my friends. I felt that I was often the butt of practical jokes. Fitting in became everything to me, and being accepted by the other kids was the ultimate achievement. I felt

Fitting in became everything to me, and being accepted by the other kids was the ultimate achievement.

that my parents were overprotective. I was known as a mama's boy, and I started to resent my family because of this.

I had a friend whose parents had divorced. He and his brothers lived a life of complete and absolute freedom from parental supervision, and for years I envied the lack of authority and discipline in their lives. This friend, on the other hand, envied the loving bond and protective environment that he witnessed while spending time with me and my family. Not until years later would I really understand his desire to be part of a nurturing and loving family such as mine—and how lucky I'd been to have had the family that I did.

But back then, not only did I begin to resent my parents for, well, being *them,* I also developed anger toward those who did not accept me. For an adolescent, the need to be accepted by the "in crowd" can be of paramount importance. In my case, this need led me down a very self-destructive path. Fitting in and escaping from my overwhelming feelings of low self-esteem were two of the major themes of my early experimentation with alcohol and drugs.

I was probably twelve when I started to really distance myself from my parents. I used them as an excuse for my low self-esteem, blaming them for my unhappiness when it was me that I truly disliked. I was pretty much a mess inside even though on the outside I was holding it together. I was ill at ease and dissatisfied with my life. Basically, I felt that I was destined to be incompatible with the world around me, and the feelings of self-loathing continued to grow until, in high school, I found what I thought was my first opportunity to escape them.

A Forbidden Sip

When I was a teenager, there was a bar in town that all the underage kids could get into, and everybody knew about it.

My affair with illegal substances began there with a simple sip of beer, followed by another, each one taking me further and further away from the boy who loved to play in the woods and go on fishing trips with his father. Alcohol had never been taboo in our family—instead, it had been present in our home all my life. My father came from a big family that liked to have fun, and they had many parties—Memorial Day, Labor Day, Fourth of July. These events always involved alcohol for the adults, but I've never known any of my relatives to be alcoholics or problem drinkers. For me, of course, it would be different.

It was at this same bar, one night when I was 16, that I remember experiencing the full effects of alcohol for the first time. I wasn't drinking beer, but grain alcohol, 180-proof (this means that whatever I was drinking was about 90% alcohol; most beers and wines are around 5% to 7%, so you can imagine how strong that stuff was). I was an extremist from the very beginning. I got drunk that night and loved it. I enjoyed the feeling of being able to unleash my inhibitions, while at the same time somehow detach from myself. I thought that first night that I had found a way to escape my own unpleasant reality. I embraced this realization with everything I had and was quickly swept up into a whirlpool of self-destructive behavior that would eventually carry me spiraling into misery and isolation.

During this same period, I underwent a kind of social metamorphosis. I had entered high school as a timid, shy, introverted kid who was made fun of a lot, and I didn't fit in with anybody. But when I had that first experience with alcohol and followed it up with many similar experiences, I came to believe that if I drank, I became more sociable, more likable—not only to others, but to myself as well. I felt untouchable. For some reason, I didn't like to feel strong emotions—maybe because most of the strong emotions I did feel at that time in my life were negative.

Drinking seemed to make all my bad feelings go away. Alcohol allowed me to not feel, not think—just to escape. My whole life became about escaping. At first, alcohol had been about superficial things like socializing and partying, but underneath all that was the way it took me away from myself, or changed me into somebody who was more comfortable inside his own skin.

At the time, strange as it may seem now, I was against drugs. In fact, I wanted to become an undercover police officer. My favorite TV program was the cop show *21 Jump Street,* which made law enforcement and police work seem hip and cool. When I heard that a few of my friends had tried pot, I was angry, though I have to admit it also intrigued me. It was something so taboo, and yet that feeling of fear and intrigue was so enticing.

It was something so taboo, and yet that feeling of fear and intrigue was so enticing.

Around this time I also started to become interested in philosophy and existentialism. I considered one of my favorite musicians, Jim Morrison of The Doors, to be a true philosophical thinker. I started to read a lot. I'd never read before except when I had to for my high school classes. But once I read a biography of Morrison, my whole perspective on education and reading and enlightenment changed. I had considered myself to be kind of goofy and not very bright, but once I started to read about Morrison and all the people *he* read about, I moved on to Nietzsche and Schopenhauer and Kierkegaard. I can remember trying to get through the *Critique of Pure Reason,* by Immanuel Kant. Learning about Jim

Morrison's life also softened up my attitude toward drugs. It's generally accepted that Morrison died of a heroin overdose, but that didn't seem to matter to me at the time.

Of course, I had heard the stories about drugs, and I had told myself I'd never get involved with that stuff. But the material I was reading, plus the pressure from friends, and a certain interest inspired by things that were so forbidden were gradually beginning to change my attitude. Plus, I'd been excited and inspired by the stories of someone who to me was the greatest drug addict who ever lived, Jim Morrison. When I finally decided to try smoking marijuana for the first time, I couldn't actually get any to smoke. Only a couple of people I knew had tried it, but it was starting to make its way into our crowd.

One Puff Leads to Another

The first time I got high on pot was with some friends whose mother was a pot smoker. I thought it was wonderful and once I smoked it, I had to smoke it every day. It had been the same with drinking—once I drank, I had to drink every day. So now, every day, I would talk my way out of school early, and friends and I would go get some forty-ounce bottles of malt liquor and some marijuana, and we would find somebody's house whose parents were at work, and we would sit around and get intoxicated. It was a daily event.

I thought it was all in good fun, but my identity now revolved around my consumption of chemicals. I was known as the guy who could handle constantly smoking all that pot and drinking all that alcohol as an everyday thing. That's how I built my reputation and started to become popular. Or at least that's what I thought then.

In my small town and for my group of friends, substances came in waves. It wasn't like in New York City, where one could go out and get whatever one wanted. In our town, we were limited to whatever was around at the time and the group always took it together. When pot was available, we'd smoke it. When pharmaceuticals were available, we'd take those, too— Valium, Lithium, Seconal, Vicodin, and Percocet. I don't know if I was physically dependent yet, but I had a psychological dependence without a doubt.

While all this was going on, an important decision was approaching for me—what I would do when I finished high school. My father had always told me stories about when he was in the Navy, and one day he told me about Navy SEALs, who were the elite, top-of-the-spectrum, the apex of the special forces. Part of me wanted to be a Navy SEAL, but part of me wanted to be a neo-hippie drug addict, an enlightened Timothy Leary type, because LSD was coming into the picture next.

I wondered, do I become the straight, disciplined, military figure or do I just give in to the drugs and let everything in my life get crazy? Am I the type of person who would prefer everyone love each other or would I be able to kill if ordered to? Would I even be able to become a Navy SEAL? I felt this conflict inside of me about who I really was, and what direction I was going to take after high school.

I felt this conflict inside of me about who I really was, and what direction I was going to take after high school.

These questions nagged at me as LSD became the next wave of drugs to be eagerly consumed by me and my friends. In the beginning, I remember taking such tiny pieces that I wouldn't feel it. I told people that I had tripped on acid even though I hadn't actually felt the famous psychedelic effects of the drug.

Finally I took enough to have my first trip. I don't remember the details of that day, but LSD became a major part of my life during the eleventh and twelfth grades. I took it multiple times a week. I had what I thought were revelations in understanding, even moments of enlightenment. But I also would see people jump through windows, see demons, and go completely (if temporarily) insane.

By now I had become adept at manipulating people, and I felt I was in the upper echelon socially at school. I had friends in every category—popular kids, jocks, nerds, skateboarders, punk rockers, metal heads, and mid-grade kids who weren't popular or unpopular. I rode a skateboard, I listened to punk rock music, I had long hair, I did drugs, and I was athletic. I was a well-known, popular person. But I also knew that at least part of it was a sham. It was me saying things that people wanted or expected to hear, and doing things and manipulating people to do what I wanted them to do. I was playing a part, pretending to be something on the outside when on the inside, all I felt was emptiness. I continued to try and fill that emptiness with chemicals.

I had a few close calls in those early days of using, but nothing so serious as to make me stop. One night I smoked some marijuana without knowing that it was laced with PCP, and I became a quivering, paranoid pile of just nothing. Other nights I would take LSD with my friends, and one of them would have a bad trip and I would have to act as the caretaker.

There were many times that I had to care for other people and, strangely, nothing felt better than to act like a leader in this way. All I had to do was say things that people wanted to hear. It worked like a charm. I could easily convince people to see things my way, which turned out to be a useful trait later on in my life as an addict. I was sharpening my skills as a master manipulator.

My Uncertain Future

By the time I graduated from high school, I still had no idea where to go or what to do. I thought about going to college and eventually becoming a psychologist or a psychiatrist because I had that ability to know people's minds and predict what they were going to do. But I also continued to be fascinated by the military field manuals and with the idea of being in the Navy.

I finally decided to join the Navy, hoping someday to become a Navy SEAL. I even managed to quit smoking pot for a month so I'd pass the military's mandatory drug test. As soon as basic training in San Diego was over, though, I realized I'd made a mistake. I was having serious difficulties adjusting to life away from my friends and family, and I did not enjoy the discipline and lack of freedom associated with military life. Moreover, my ambition to join the SEALs was shattered when I learned that my eyesight did not meet the standards that would allow me to be considered for Navy SEAL boot camp. I spent most of my free time drinking and hooking up my Navy friends with LSD, the only drug we believed to be undetectable by the standard drug tests. After a while, I guess my poor performance and behavior caught up with me, and I was discharged for psychological reasons. On the day of my departure I received a letter from my parents telling me how proud they were of my decision to join the Navy, and how sure they were that I would succeed. But it was too late. I returned home to the East Coast humiliated and ashamed.

Just as I was leaving the Navy, I had my first experience with crystal methamphetamine. Out west, meth was a big epidemic.

I sniffed one line and I loved it. I couldn't understand why people thought it was so bad. I didn't realize how dangerous and highly addictive it is. I experienced that later on, but this first time I thought it was the greatest thing ever. When I got out of the Navy, I bought some and brought it back home with me on the train to New York. I was excited to get home to see my friends, but I also knew that my parents were going to be really disappointed. My shame fueled the discontent I felt just being in my own skin.

Things hadn't changed much in my hometown while I was away, except for one thing. A few of my friends were now experimenting with cocaine. It didn't take much convincing for me to jump right on that bandwagon. I was ready to accept anything that would make me feel like I was coping with my recent failure. The first time I tried cocaine, it opened me up socially. I came down after a little while and went to sleep. I wondered what all the hype was about, and did it a few more times.

I was ready to accept anything that would make me feel like I was coping with my recent failure.

In the meantime, to make up for my unsuccessful attempt at military life, I decided to attend the local community college for liberal arts and pursue a secondary education in psychology, in line with my interest in human behavior and the human mind. But college turned into a bust. I didn't take classes seriously. Drugs and partying were a full-time job and they left little room for academics. After the first semester, I dropped out. Because of drugs, everything else in my life was steadily deteriorating, too. Cocaine was now a nightly activity, and every morning as I lay in bed calculating how much money I had wasted the night before, I sank deeper and deeper into a state of depression. The withdrawal from cocaine had become more and more punishing, and taking even the slightest bit now would send me spiraling into an abyss of paranoia, anxiety, fear, and frustration. My mood had become callous and indifferent. My friends who didn't use drugs began to distance themselves from me. I knew something needed to be done, and quickly.

I started seeing a girl I had dated in high school. We agreed to try to remain clean and free from all mind-altering substances, but this only lasted a short time. Soon I was back at it, full force, and she was right there with me. Everything was falling apart. We broke up shortly thereafter. Again, I felt like a failure and my depression worsened.

The following weeks were filled with emotional and psychological pain. I could not swallow enough intoxicants to suppress this suffering. Life had become meaningless and I wandered around aimlessly from day to day. I took a job as a security guard. Sitting in that booth alone all night just gave me more time to focus on my failures and strengthen my self-hatred. Then, one weekend I got a call from a friend who told me he had a surprise for me and I should stop by. Had I known what was about to happen, and the profound effect it would have on the next several years of my life, I surely would have kept driving. As my friend and I sat in his living room, he handed me a plastic bag containing a small amount of white powder.

Heroin

Once in high school, I was sitting in the lunch room with some friends and we were talking about drugs, and I remember saying that if I was in the right situation and with somebody trustworthy, I would let him inject me with heroin. Heroin was the ultimate, the most forbidden, the deadliest, the most dangerous, and I have to be honest and admit that this was enticing to me. I remember an episode of *21 Jump Street*—ironically, the same show that had sparked my interest in becoming a cop—in which Johnny Depp goes undercover in a school. There's a student who shoots heroin, and after school he goes to this little clubhouse where he reads and writes poetry. I felt I could identify with that. I thought I was a writer, a poet and a reader, an intellect. Heroin seemed like a romantic conquest of the ultimate experience with the dark side of life.

Years later, when my friend actually did offer me heroin, I was so filled with despair from the loss of my girlfriend, plus the seemingly ceaseless string of personal and professional failures since high school, that I didn't care about anything. I was so miserable that I would've swallowed turpentine if I'd thought it would stop the pain. It never occurred to me that there might be other solutions to my problems, like counseling. So there was no hesitation. I took the heroin and did it all right there. Suddenly, the pain was gone. As the drug began to take effect, I felt all of my worries slip away. It was like being enveloped in a shower of medicinal bliss. I immediately realized that this type of high would not come without a price, but I didn't realize just exactly what it would cost me until much later.

Although for a while now I had been abusing alcohol, marijuana, LSD, and cocaine, I had never really considered myself an addict (which, in fact, I was, since I relied on these drugs to get me through the day and to avoid withdrawal). But I discarded those substances as soon as I was introduced to heroin. I had to make some changes to incorporate this new vice into my lifestyle. I started selling heroin to support my own use. I abandoned all my pastimes as well as any and all friends who opposed my using. My parents immediately saw that something extremely wrong was happening; I don't think they realized the extent of my problem, though, and they certainly didn't know what to do about it.

It took only about three months for me to become totally addicted to heroin. Unlike the few friends of mine who were treading the same path, I never denied my dependence on the substance and openly declared myself an addict to fellow users. I was proud of myself. All the antidrug programs at school, all the after-school specials against drugs, all the admonitions by authority figures, the stigma, the reputation, the horror stories, all of it was no match for what I was feeling, and I wanted more.

A Rite of Passage Versus the Slippery Slope to Addiction

My introduction (and later, addiction) to heroin is part of a much bigger picture surrounding the hows and whys of substance abuse and addiction in our society. First, some details from my past are worth repeating. There was nothing all that unusual about my family or my early life that could predict my future as a drug addict. My childhood and adolescence were stable and healthy. We weren't poor and I didn't suffer any kind of abuse or neglect. I went to good schools. No slums and no gangs or other criminal elements mar my background. I started out, in other words, as a pretty ordinary kid in a pretty ordinary family, neighborhood, and school. My friends, both those who later went on to use drugs and those who did not, started out pretty ordinary, too.

These details may seem irrelevant, but they do tell us something very important about the relationship between drug and alcohol use and young people in American society today. These days, in most parts of the country, the use of alcohol and drugs by teenagers is fairly unexceptional. Experimentation with substances is not weird or freakish, nor something that only the "bad" or "disturbed" kids do. The truth is that a number of young people from all kinds of backgrounds experiment with drugs and alcohol, and in doing so they are exhibiting some of the natural curiosity that comes along with being a perfectly normal teenager. For the vast majority of young people, this experimentation will not lead to addiction, and they will eventually leave such behaviors behind as they grow into adulthood.

> The truth is that a number of young people from all kinds of backgrounds experiment with drugs and alcohol ...

For example, in 2002 the University of Michigan's Monitoring the Future study revealed that one in four eighth graders (25%) in the United States had tried some illegal drug, and that over half (53%) had done so by high school graduation. After alcohol, the substance that kids most commonly used was marijuana. About 10% of eighth graders and 40% of twelfth graders, for example, did so in 2002.

As for alcohol, it is the most commonly used psychoactive (meaning mind-altering) substance among teens. Legally available nearly everywhere to those over 21, it is present in millions of American homes—including mine, and perhaps yours, too. It also carries something of a special status: Obtaining the right and privilege to buy and drink alcohol legally is one of the marks of becoming an adult in this country. It is also advertised everywhere, and as television watchers, magazine readers, and movie goers, we're relentlessly pelted with images selling the idea that alcohol consumption is cool, grown-up, and safe. So with its status and its availability, maybe it's no surprise that kids trying to act grown-up want to use it, too. It is of course illegal for them to obtain it, but for most, that is a minor technicality. Think of the bar in my home town that I mentioned earlier, the one where at age 16 I happily knocked back 180-proof, no questions asked. There are lots of places like that, and lots of ways for underage kids to get booze. In fact, about 80% of high school students have at least tried alcohol by their senior year.

Teenage use of drugs and alcohol is common enough that a sociologist, somebody who studies human society and its structures and processes, might say that in much of middle-class America, it is *normal* and even *normative.* By *normal,* sociologists mean that enough people are participating in an activity that it should not be considered unusual. By *normative,* they mean that the activity is part of the usual or standard way that people in a certain group—in this case, American teenagers—believe that they are permitted or expected to behave. (Note that just because a sociologist considers a given activity to be normal or normative does not mean that the activity isn't also harmful.) Many consider a small amount of experimentation with drugs to be a rite of passage for young people, or simply a part of growing up.

For lots of young people—and I was no exception—using alcohol or drugs seems to form part of the all-important transition to early adulthood, not only because drinking plays such an important role in adult social life but also because using drugs and alcohol illegally is a form of rebellion. Most of the kids who drink or use drugs do move on, to college or work, or maybe to the military like I did. And most eventually begin their lives as adults without any major difficulties caused by their dabbling in substances.

So far so good, right? The problem is that a few young people do slip into chronic substance abuse to the point where it engulfs them. You know enough about my own experience so far to know that's what happened to me; I used many substances until finally heroin became my drug of choice. In fact, heroin use among young people has increased since 1992, and I was just one person caught up in that wave. Among those who try heroin, about 22% become addicted. While half of all high school graduates have tried an illegal drug, only about 0.2% of 12- to 17-year-olds are heroin users. As my addiction progressed, I became a member of a minority of people whose experimentation led to distressingly active and repetitive use, and then to addiction.

The Ride Down That Slope

Figuring out why my experimentation turned into addiction isn't a simple matter. What I know is that on the road from experimentation to full-blown addiction, I passed through different stages. There aren't hard-and-fast boundaries separating them, and not everyone moves along the road at the same rate. In fact, some people proceed only a certain distance and then stay there, whereas others, like me, go the whole way. The stages, roughly divided, are experimentation, hazardous use, and addiction.

Figuring out why my experimentation turned into addiction isn't a simple matter.

Experimentation

I just talked about this, but it's worth emphasizing: During the experimental stage, individuals engage in occasional drug use that has not yet had a major impact on their lives. Using drugs is a voluntary decision, and deciding not to use is still feasible. The brain has not undergone significant adaptation to the substance, so neither psychological nor physical dependence has yet been established. A relatively small amount of the substance is still adequate to produce the desired response—to get high. It is at this stage that many teenagers feel they must try a certain drug in order to fit in, or to avoid being rejected by friends who use. Kids may want to use the substance again because they enjoyed some aspect of the experience, but they do not yet experience a physical compulsion or urge to use. You can see this dynamic in my first experience with alcohol, marijuana, and heroin. I used all of these drugs voluntarily, even though I knew this was not a wise idea. I kept using them because I enjoyed the reputation earned by all that drug use, and I didn't think I would fall victim to addiction.

Hospital Trip

No two people progress from experimentation to hazardous use to addiction in exactly the same way; my early experiences with drugs may look quite different from yours, and both of our stories might differ dramatically from another person's. In *Rolling Away*, Lynn Marie Smith tells of her addiction to the club drug ecstasy and of how her life as an acting student in New York City was nearly cut short by it. In this passage, she describes the horror of her first experience with LSD.

I was handcuffed to a bed in Bellevue Hospital. I was in a bright room, too bright, all white, blinding. Masked men were hovering above me. I couldn't see any faces, just eyes. One had a needle, which became a knife, and he began poking at my right arm. Even though I was handcuffed to the bed, I tried desperately to move my arm away from him. I felt a stabbing pain. I was just a little speck in the center of all of this. I had no control. It was like Lynn, the real Lynn, was locked inside, waiting to be let out. Another one of them told me to drink a cup of thick, liquid tar. I refused. They jabbed tubes into my nose that turned into snakes. Liquid flooded my head, my brain, and my throat. I gagged over and over and over until I passed out. (Reprinted from Lynn Marie Smith, *Rolling Away: My Agony with Ecstasy* [New York: Atria Books, 2005].)

Hazardous Use

As experimentation progresses, the level of usage increases and its harmful effects become noticeable and progressively more problematic. Gradually the amount taken may increase because more of the drug is needed to produce the same effect. As I mentioned, this is called *tolerance,* and it's a sign that changes in the brain caused by drug use are well underway. Users may think about the substance quite a lot, and may start to feel cravings for it. The negative consequences of substance use begin to pile up: slipping grades, loss of interest in activities and hobbies, getting into trouble of various kinds, accidents, bad decisions. Old friends may start to drift away and new ones start appearing. You can see this pattern in my story, too; I started using more and more drugs as I became more and more unhappy in my life. Finally I tried heroin because none of the other drugs could erase the pain I was feeling. I'd quit the Navy and dropped out of college because of drugs and alcohol, not realizing these actions indicated that substances were taking over my life.

Addiction

When the use of the substance has become a chronic and relapsing disease that has taken control of the person's brain and life, an addiction has been established. An addict can no longer cease use of the drug without suffering the physical effects of withdrawal, and large amounts of the drug are required to elicit the drug's psychological effects. At the height of my addiction, I could not bear to go more than a few hours without using heroin, and I turned to all sorts of delinquent and criminal behaviors to support my habit. When I did go without the drug for an extended period, I suffered agonizing withdrawal and depression. All considerations for my family and friends, right and wrong, faded into the distance, completely blotted out by my need for heroin.

Who Becomes Addicted, Who Does Not, and Why?

Why some people become addicted to substances and others do not is a mystery that scientists have yet to fully solve. Lots of scientific studies suggest that no single element in one's life can account for addiction. Rather, the process involves a mix of factors, and which ones are most important probably varies among individuals. These characteristics raise risk—they don't determine behavior. It's very complicated, and to complicate things more, even if a person does appear to have one or more of the risk factors, that does not guarantee that he or she will use drugs or become addicted. A person could be at risk from every direction and still come out okay, reaching adulthood without having used drugs. On the flip side, another person may seem to have escaped all of these risk factors but still wind up troubled by an addiction. What is clear is that the factors that increase the risk of drug use in adolescents include biology, genetics, social pressures, and psychological issues, as well as environment and personal experience. In general, when a person becomes addicted, chances are good that some or all of the following factors come into play.

...the factors that increase the risk of drug use in adolescents include biology, genetics, social pressures, and psychological issues, as well as environment and personal experience.

Biology

Addiction is a biological process based on the way the human brain is built. I'll have much more to say about this in the next chapter, but the short of it here is that at a molecular level, addictive substances are structured in such a way that they can take advantage of some of the brain's natural features. A number of these drugs are themselves naturally occurring substances that just happen to fit in with how our brains work. Others are synthetic chemicals specifically devised with the intention of invading and affecting the human brain.

Whatever a drug's origin, however, if it is addictive, it works through our biology to alter the way particular parts of our brains function. Doing this allows the drug to change—sometimes temporarily, but sometimes permanently—how we feel, perceive, think, and act. Oftentimes these alterations produce experiences that users find enjoyable, with feelings of relaxation or euphoria or omnipotence, with distortions of the senses that make the world seem magical or exciting. These pleasurable feelings naturally lead some users to want to use over and over again, which can quickly lead to drug addiction. This happens because the substance can hijack an important functional area of the user's brain.

Once addicted, people suffer from another of addiction's hallmarks, withdrawal symptoms. These take the form of great physical or emotional discomfort whenever the person can't get the substance, and are specific to the drug of abuse. Withdrawal from opiates, for instance, may be accompanied by muscle aches, tearing, running nose, sweats, diarrhea, fever, and insomnia. Withdrawal from alcohol is often marked by agitation, tremors, elevated pulse and blood pressure, and delirium. The need to avoid unpleasant withdrawal symptoms is another way in which drugs manipulate our biology and lead to addiction.

But what makes one person's biology more vulnerable to addiction than another's? It is believed that people with a certain brain chemistry and/or structure may have different reactions to substances than people without these traits. Drugs of abuse have both pleasurable and aversive (unpleasant) effects, and the most cutting-edge addiction science seems to indicate that people with a certain brain chemistry have a diminished response to the aversive effects—making drug use that much more enjoyable for them. Researchers believe that those who experience a higher level of enjoyment because of these traits in their brains are likelier to continue using potentially addictive substances than are those who, for biological reasons, experience less pleasure, or maybe even discomfort, from the same dose. This biologically based level of enjoyment would obviously increase the risk of addiction later on.

Age and Age at the Time of First Use

Scientists used to think that the adolescent brain was pretty much the same as the adult brain; they assumed that by puberty, brain chemistry and structure were established and would not continue to develop throughout adolescence. Now we know that view is wrong. Brain imaging technologies such as magnetic resonance imaging (MRI) and positron emission tomography (PET) scanning have shown that the brain continues to develop well into adolescence. Research has proven that, because their brains are still developing, adolescents are not as adept at handling things like social pressure, impulsive urges, and other stressful situations as adults are. Not surprisingly, this renders teens much more susceptible to risky behavior like experimentation with drugs. Obviously, no one can become addicted to drugs without actually using them, so adolescents' predisposition to take risks and experiment with drugs in the first place is a potent risk factor for addiction.

Other studies have shown that the earlier a kid first tries drugs or alcohol, the more likely he or she is to develop substance abuse later on. This is why antidrug activists and agencies focus so heavily on preventing even the most harmless-seeming early experimentation with drugs and alcohol. These behaviors may seem harmless at first, but statistically speaking, they greatly increase the risk of an addiction.

Genetics

Scientists have conducted numerous studies that show that, all other things being equal (like environment, availability of drugs, age, and so on) some people are generally more vulnerable to addiction than others. The explosion in genetic research over the past few decades has led to some interesting conclusions about how a person's genes affect his or her vulnerability to addiction.

First off, we know that addiction has a genetic component because it has a tendency to run in families.

First off, we know that addiction has a genetic component because it has a tendency to run in families. Naturally, this could result from the fact that family members tend to share experiences and live in similar environments. But a type of research known as *cross-adoption studies* has revealed that there's more to the story. Children born to alcoholic parents but who were adopted at birth and raised by non-alcoholic adoptive parents were still four times more likely to develop alcoholism than were their non-adopted, non-biological siblings. Other studies with fraternal and identical twins tell a similar tale. Identical twins share identical DNA (and, by extension, the same genes) while fraternal twins share only half of the same genes. Research has shown that the identical twin of an addict is much more likely to also be addicted than is the fraternal twin of an addict. These findings clearly indicate that people can inherit a predisposition to addiction no matter what their environmental surroundings look like.

Clearly, a person's genetic endowment can play a key role in their vulnerability to addiction. That doesn't mean, however, that if a person is predisposed toward addiction that he or she will *definitely* become an addict. As with the other risk factors discussed here, genetic heritage is only part of the package, and often must be combined with other risk factors to spark an addiction. Furthermore, one need not have a genetic predisposition toward addictive disorders to become addicted to anything; about half of all people with an addiction come from families where no genetic transmission is evident.

Social Relationships and Environment

As you've seen in my story so far, use of addictive substances generally happens within a web of social relationships. One of the reasons I first started using alcohol and drugs, for example, was that I felt doing so increased my social stature among people I considered cool. I liked the reputation I earned with those people as a fellow user. It stands to reason that if I'd valued the opinions and friendships of non-using friends and classmates, I wouldn't have been so quick to try drugs.

Research conducted by developmental scientists supports my own personal experience. It's been proven that young men often provide their male friends with the means and social pressure that eventually lead them to engage in substance abuse. On the flipside, girls who have an older or adult boyfriend are more likely to try drugs and alcohol at an early age. Though girls and boys go through different developmental stages and experience different social pressures, it's clear that the people we pick as our friends and companions have a tremendous effect on whether we'll try drugs and/or alcohol and, by extension, increase our risk of an addiction.

Some relationships seem to lessen the risk of addiction. Kids who are close to their parents are less likely to engage in risky substance use, as are kids whose friends practice abstinence. In fact, the presence of any positive and supportive adult role model in an adolescent's life, whether a parent, a coach, a member of the clergy, or an adult sibling, can help protect that adolescent from engaging in reckless behavior. Conversely, kids who grow up with parents and other adults who engage in problematic use of substances are more likely to develop a substance abuse problem themselves. Furthermore, when parents are absent from the home frequently and young people are unsupervised, they're more likely to engage in dangerous substance use. Similarly, a young person's risk for a substance abuse problem can be increased if he or she lives in a neighborhood that is rife with drug use.

Young people who are religious are less likely to become drug addicts, as are those who participate in healthy extracurricular activities like sports. Remember me and my friends, in that empty house, smoking pot and drinking after school every day? Chances are that if we'd had soccer or football practice to go to, or rehearsal for a play, or another constructive after-school activity, we wouldn't have gotten so involved with drugs.

Emotional and Psychological Issues

Many young people who use addictive substances are also afflicted with what are known as *comorbid* (or co-occurring) mental health conditions. It is sometimes difficult to know whether these conditions are a cause or a result of the chemical abuse, but it's clear to scientists that the presence of a psychiatric illness increases the risk that an adolescent will abuse drugs. Some kids use them in a doomed attempt to self-medicate, using substances to find emotional and/ or psychological escape from the painful symptoms of a mental disorder.

...the presence of a psychiatric illness increases the risk that an adolescent will abuse drugs.

The mental health disorders that are often found to affect teens who abuse drugs including the following:

- *Mood disorders*
  Depression and *bipolar disorder* (also known as manic depression) are two major mood disorders that may co-occur in young people with substance abuse problems. Depression is characterized by feelings of sadness and/ or emptiness and loss of interest in activities, and may be accompanied by significant weight loss, sleep problems, feelings of worthlessness or guilt, and recurring thoughts of death or suicide. Depression is thought to occur in as many as 14% of adolescents. Bipolar disorder, on the other hand, causes intense mood swings that cycle between depression and mania (high energy and feelings of invincibility and grandiosity). At its most severe, bipolar disorder can be extremely impairing and even cause psychosis. Studies suggest that anywhere from 1% to 6% of adolescents suffer from some form of bipolar disorder. Young people who are depressed may turn to drugs, alcohol, and cigarettes in an attempt to ease their emotional pain, and substance abuse in

adolescents increases the risk of suicide; bipolar teenagers may use drugs to help quell violent mood swings.

- *Anxiety disorders*
  There are many types of anxiety disorders, four of which
  are social anxiety disorder, in which the sufferer fears
  certain social situations; generalized anxiety disorder, in
  which a person feels fear or worry over a wide range of
  situations or objects; obsessive-compulsive disorder, in
  which a person must repeat certain rituals or mantras to
  quell rising anxiety; and post-traumatic stress disorder
  (PTSD), in which a person feels overwhelming fear and
  anxiety associated with the trauma of some past event.
  Anxiety can range from mildly troubling to debilitat-
  ing, and is quite common among adolescents; about
  one in twenty young people, or 5%, are thought to
  have some type of anxiety disorder.

  Much research has been done on the relationship between anxiety disorders and substance abuse, but the
  link is still not entirely clear. Scientists do know that
  kids with generalized anxiety disorder are more likely to
  drink alcohol than their peers, and to do so at a younger
  age. Adolescents with PTSD are especially prone to substance abuse, perhaps because of the added risk factor
  of a trauma in their past; one study found that 46% of
  young people with this anxiety disorder became dependent on alcohol by the age of 18, and 25% became
  dependent on other drugs.

- *Schizophrenia*
  Schizophrenia is a severe mental illness characterized
  by the disintegration of the thinking process, of emotional responsiveness, and of contact with reality. It
  can cause delusions and hallucinations. People with

schizophrenia are more likely to use illegal substances than most other people, and are most likely to be addicted to cigarettes—one study found that between 75% and 90% of people with schizophrenia smoke. This could be because nicotine reduces some of the anxiety felt by those with this difficult illness, while also improving concentration.

Silencing Voices

Lori Schiller was an ordinary kid with a loving family, just like I was. She was just 17 when she began to hear voices that urged her to commit acts of violence and self-harm. Diagnosed with schizoaffective disorder, a blend of schizophrenia and a mood disorder, Schiller was in and out of hospitals and treatment programs for over seven years. In this passage from her book *The Quiet Room,* she describes how cocaine temporarily relieved her symptoms, leading her to an addiction just as tenacious and unforgiving as my own.

All I wanted was to feel better. Those medications they gave me in the hospital were useless. I took them because people told me they would make me better. But lots of times I didn't know why I bothered. They only thing those fistfuls of stupid pills did was make me feel fuzzy and disoriented, as if I were at the bottom of a swimming pool. And the Voices still raged away at me, mocking the drugs, the doctors and me.

Cocaine, on the other hand, helped me ignore the Voices. For as long as it lasted, cocaine made me feel alive. It made my senses feel sharp and clear again. When I did a line, I felt good, I felt real, I felt vital in a way I hadn't since long before the Voices entered my life. Cocaine directed my attention outside of myself. As long as I was high, I had enough strength to ignore those Voices calling me back into their world.

So for a while I found the relief I wanted. When the crash came as it always did, I went back for more. When the crashes came closer together, the search for relief began to consume

(continued)

more of my time and my life. Before too long, the search for cocaine—and of ways of getting it—began to be the single-minded focus of my existence. (Reprinted from Lori Schiller, *The Quiet Room* [New York: Grand Central Publishing, 1996].)

Schiller became mentally ill at a time when many of the pharmaceutical treatments for schizoaffective disorder were inadequate or produced devastating side effects. She eventually broke free of her addiction when her doctors prescribed a newer antipsychotic medication that suppressed her symptoms more effectively than older drugs, and which had less severe side effects.

Perhaps more troubling, though, is the idea that some psychoactive substances, like marijuana or hallucinogens, can actually trigger schizophrenia in certain individuals. Young people who may be predisposed to schizophrenia (such as those with a family member who has the illness) should be particularly aware of this risk when contemplating experimenting with drugs.

- *Eating disorders*
  Anorexia nervosa and *bulimia nervosa* are two psychiatric illnesses characterized by severe disturbances in eating behavior, such as excessive dieting to the point of starvation, overexercising, binge eating, or purging. In anorexia nervosa, body weight falls well below normal and all sorts of physical and emotional problems follow, including heart irregularities, anemia, weak bones, and anxiety and depression. Bulimia nervosa is also associated with anxiety and depression, but physical problems are typically not as severe as those associated with anorexia nervosa because weight is usually normal. Young people with eating disorders, especially those with bulimia, have some tendency to abuse substances, especially alcohol, cocaine, and marijuana.

- *Attention-deficit hyperactivity disorder*
  Attention-deficit hyperactivity disorder (ADHD) is a childhood mental disorder that affects about three times as many boys as girls. ADHD is characterized by persistent inattention, hyperactivity, and/or impulsivity that negatively affect functioning at home and at school. It is usually treated with stimulant medication, but scientists are currently investigating medications that can be used for individuals who have both ADHD and a substance abuse problem. Drug abuse has been shown to occur more frequently in adolescents who have a history of ADHD than in those who do not.
- *Conduct disorder*
  Conduct disorder refers to a series of emotional and behavioral problems that afflict some young people. Kids with conduct disorder may have difficulty following rules and behaving in socially acceptable ways. This troubling psychiatric illness often manifests in aggression toward people or animals, destruction of property and vandalism, deceitfulness, and theft. In the 1950s, kids with conduct disorder were called "juvenile delinquents" because of their petty criminal activity.

> ...a high rate of adolescents with substance abuse problems also have a history of conduct disorder...

Studies have shown that a high rate of adolescents with substance abuse problems also have a history of conduct disorder, and the illness can seriously complicate substance abuse treatment. Behavior therapy is often used in treating conduct disorder, and the earlier someone receives treatment for it, the more positive the outcome.

Trauma, Abuse, and Neglect

Research has shown that adolescents who have suffered a trauma, or who have been abused or neglected by a trusted adult, are more likely to abuse substances. Drugs of abuse can temporarily blunt bad feelings and stress, so it's possible that people seeking to escape from bad experiences in their past may be more susceptible to drug use because of the relief, even if short-lived, that it can bring.

Availability

Another important risk factor is whether or not drugs are even available. Nobody, regardless of his or her genes, biology, or social situation, can become addicted unless addictive substances get into the body. In my home town, for example, I could only use what the crowd was using. Clearly, young people who live in situations where lots of addictive substances are available have a greater risk of becoming addicted than those who live in more drug-free environments.

These are the main risk factors scientifically known to contribute to addiction. Unfortunately, despite having identified them, researchers still have a lot of unanswered questions about how these risk factors interact with each other, why they affect some individuals more deeply than others, and how some or all of them can be avoided to prevent addiction. Furthermore, most of the research on risk factors has been conducted using adult addicts, and in many cases scientists have been forced to theorize that their conclusions extend to adolescents as well. Fortunately, research to learn more about the risks for drug abuse in adolescents is increasing, so in time scientists will know a lot more than they do now about prevention and avoidance of addiction in this age group.

For now, if you're one of the many young people exposed to enough risk that you've engaged in harmful drug use, you may not want to see or accept that you have a problem—or if you do, you may think that you can't do anything about it. If so, I've been where you are, and I know it's a desolate place. Read on, and let me tell you about my experience of that place—if only so I can show you a way out of it.

Chapter Three

The Noose Tightens

When I think now about the early days of my heroin use (something I try not to do too often), it seems like it all happened only yesterday—the memories are that clear. At twenty I was already traveling regularly into Manhattan to buy the drug. I was sniffing two to three bags a day, and this had been going on for about a month and a half. But then something changed. On one particular trip to the city with three other users, I was feeling a little under the weather—a bit of a chill, a few stomach cramps, and a persistent feeling of sadness and aloneness. I figured I was coming down with a cold. The chills grew worse, and then came the cold sweats, not unbearable but quite uncomfortable. And then it happened. We bought the drugs and quickly sniffed. All of a sudden, it was as if someone had breathed life into me, replenished my spirit, my vitality. Immediately my symptoms were gone.

A Moment of Truth, and Then Denial

In that moment I realized that I had arrived: I was addicted. I acknowledged something else as well—that I was chasing something more than the high. I was chasing release from the sickness of withdrawal that came when I didn't have the drug. I was chasing the transition from what felt like the brink of death to the highest euphoria, the ability of the drug to eliminate pain and deliver pleasure.

And yet, while the drug had completely taken over my life, I still didn't understand the incredible power it had to destroy me, along with everything I cared about. My life was on an even steeper downward course than it had been before. But instead of realizing that I needed professional help in overcoming the addiction, I decided I needed more heroin. And in time I decided to switch from sniffing to injecting the drug. This started with two high school classmates who worked at the factory where I'd gotten a job. These were the people I chose to inject me with heroin for the first time, before Thanksgiving dinner, at my grandmother's house. Through them, I also met several other users in the area.

Most of them were older than I was, older than I am now in fact—in their mid-thirties—and they'd been using for quite a while. They were in rough shape, some with HIV, AIDS, or Hepatitis C. Once I visited someone living in a small trailer. He was incapacitated, immobilized on the couch, unable to function because he was in withdrawal from not having his heroin. I gave him some, and he went into the bathroom and came back out a new man, completely full of energy. But he pulled me aside and said, "Look, you've got to stop doing this stuff. You don't want to end up this way. You've got to stop." I just shrugged him off. I thought I was immune to the dreadful effects that heroin had on everyone else.

I thought I was immune to the dreadful effects that heroin had on everyone else.

But of course I was wrong. I would soon leave the factory. I couldn't go to work unless I had heroin, so I'd miss days when

I couldn't get some. My work ethic was really bad. I worked on an assembly line producing lipstick, and my job was to cap the lipsticks as they went by on a conveyor belt. I'd fall asleep and a hundred lipsticks would go by uncapped. I got another job driving a van for a canoe livery on the Delaware River. I probably put people in danger with my inability to function correctly. It wasn't very long before I screwed up that job as well.

Around this time, I got caught with drugs by my parents and had my first—albeit brief—experience with any kind of treatment. I had just come home from work and I could tell immediately that something was up. My father said, "Your mother was in your room today and she found something. You know what it is, right?"

"Yes, I know what it is."

"I want you to give me everything else that you have in there."

I had just gotten a supply from New York and I assumed that was what she had found. When I opened up my hiding place, though, it was still there. But now that was exposed and I had to give up the fresh supply. I gave them all of my paraphernalia and all of the drug that I had, and they disposed of everything.

They also made an appointment with a psychologist. But as I've mentioned, I'd become pretty good at manipulating others, so I wasn't intimidated. This lady had lots of questions, but I had all the right answers. I made it seem as if there wasn't really a problem, that I was just involved in a little harmless experimentation. I lied and told her that my problem was something that could be easily addressed and solved.

She said, "Your parents have agreed to take this in stride, but you have to do something for them. You have to go to detox." Detoxification, or "detox" for short, is the procedure where an addictive drug is removed from the body and withdrawal symptoms are managed with prescribed medications. Detox is usually the first stage in drug abuse treatment.

I was indignant. Waste seven days of my life at some dreary treatment center? But it seemed I had no choice. I was determined to get through the next seven days, but I never really had any intention of actually quitting heroin.

First Shot at Detoxification

Even though the detox center was upstate, there were a lot of people there from New York City. I told my story of shooting heroin and nodding off, and they said, "You're progressing so fast. You haven't even been using a year." These old timers had been using 25, 30 years. They told me that at the rate I was going, I'd be dead in a year. They told me I wasn't going to make it. Did I listen? No. I wasn't taking anything seriously at this point.

I still didn't fully understand just how dangerous and deadly, how cunning and how manipulative heroin is. As an addict, I believed only myself—never others who said things I didn't want to hear. I believed my own lies, my own intentions. I had convinced myself that what I said I'd do was actually what I was going to do, right up until the point when I did the exact opposite. I'd do anything that would help me to achieve my goal, which was always to get high.

And so, instead of thinking about how to overcome my addiction, I would sit in my window and stare out at Route 17, knowing that it was a straight shot to New York. As a kid, I had fallen in love with the Manhattan skyline. Of course it was beautiful to begin with, *Everything was now part of the addiction.* but now it meant something more to me. It meant heroin. The skyline was the first signal that I would soon be getting high again. It was all part of the addiction. Everything was now part of the addiction.

At the same time, all of my senses, previously dulled by drugs, came to life again while in detox. I could smell the slightest of smells, and I could see things more clearly. In contrast, when I used heroin, nothing mattered. I didn't care about sights or sounds or smells or scenarios or people or situations or feelings. Everything was numb. I didn't realize it at the time, but in trying to numb my mind against the painful aspects of my life, I was also missing out on the beauty and pleasures of life. Detox can be incredibly painful because sensations—both physical and emotional—return that one hasn't experienced in a long time. That's how I was feeling after my first detox—incredibly raw, exposed, even naked without the protective haze of the drug.

As for my parents, they were naive. Heroin was something completely new to them, and they figured after seven days in detox I'd come out just like new. But when those seven days were up and I got out of detox that first time, it was as if I'd never even gone. I declined the detox center's recommendation for aftercare—drug addiction counseling designed to help an addict stay clean. Without it, no heroin addict that I know of has ever succeeded at staying clean after a few days in detox, so I knew I was chucking any chance I had at beating heroin. In my experience, many people who go to detox in the first place are just looking for a couple of days off the street.

I went home and I had a feeling inside me that I couldn't handle—an emptiness, a feeling that something in my mind just wasn't right; it was very uncomfortable. If I had not refused aftercare, if I'd bothered to consider that there might be other solutions to this emotional discomfort besides illegal drugs, the next few years of my life might have been very different.

The very night I got out of detox, I was getting high again—I didn't stay clean even for one day. I had asked my parents if I could borrow the car (they still trusted me enough to say yes) and went to pick up my girlfriend at the time, who was also using. We headed to a dealer's house and the cycle of abuse and addiction continued. I don't know exactly when my parents realized that the detox hadn't had any lasting effect, but it couldn't have taken them long to figure it out. I can't imagine how difficult that must have been for them.

Learning the Life of an Addict

In the beginning, I didn't have to resort to theft to support my habit because I was still capable of working and of selling the drug. But I was gradually learning how to steal. I learned how people I knew would shoplift from K-Mart or the drug store and then sell the stolen items to their friends for a quick twenty or thirty dollars. I watched and learned from the older, more experienced heroin addicts, acquiring a whole new set of survival skills entirely foreign to most of society.

Living in my town made it very difficult to maintain a habit. Heroin there was expensive—twenty dollars a bag. Within months, I was up to five or ten bags a day. In the city, I'd pay about half as much, so I quickly learned I could buy 30 or 40 bags in New York, sell twenty of them back at home and still have some left over for myself. In New York, people stand out on the street and take their chances selling to whoever comes along. Upstate it's all done over telephones and door to door. I knew the people I was selling to, I knew where they lived. I would play with their children. I knew everything about them. It seemed safe.

My memories of this particular period of my life aren't too sharp, but I do know that things continued to deteriorate until my first experience with jail. One morning I took my mom's car. I don't even know if I asked to borrow it, I just happened to know where the spare key was. I took some of her jewelry, too, intending to use it as collateral to obtain just enough heroin to get me through the day.

I happened to open the glove compartment and an envelope full of cash fell out. It might have been money my parents were saving for a vacation. I grabbed forty dollars and bought myself two bags. Next I realized that if I drove to the city and bought three hundred dollars worth, I could sell off half, make all the money back, put it back in the glove compartment, and still have enough for myself. What a great plan that was!

So I drove to New York City. Long story short, I used all of the heroin myself. I dropped the car off at home and left before my parents could figure out what had happened. When they saw that the money was missing, they knew where it had gone. They decided the best thing would be to press charges and have me arrested, so they had the police come with a bench warrant to arrest me. I spent about five days in jail and went through withdrawal from heroin before I was released. I got three years probation for the charge of petty larceny and was supposed to make restitution.

Sometime after the arrest I bought some street methadone—an illegal version of a prescription drug frequently used to detoxify heroin addicts—and drank it over the course of three or four days, trying to kick my habit. I still didn't

I still didn't think I needed any help getting over heroin...

think I needed any help getting over heroin—further proof of my inability to recognize the full extent of my addiction. I was clean for my twenty-first birthday, though I did go out drinking. But that didn't last and my life became pretty chaotic. I was in and out of my parents' house, and in and out of detox. I had a job for a while as a cook at a country club. But I was also selling drugs there, to people who worked and hung out at the club. When a waitress overdosed on drugs, I decided it was time to leave.

Desperate Moves

Everything was getting worse. My sister and her boyfriend had moved to Boston and agreed to let me stay on their couch for a while until I got my life in order. Before heading to Boston, I lay on my parents' couch for a week and kicked heroin, cold turkey. I just stopped and it was awful. I headed to Boston, thinking the move might be the solution to my problems.

It had not been my first time there, having bought some heroin on a previous trip. That had not been an easy score: I'd walked around downtown Boston and then eventually to the worst part of the city before I finally found a person who sold me some. When I later moved to Boston after going cold turkey, things at first went well. I was clean for about a month and a half, though I still drank in bars. I got work and an apartment and continued to stay clean for another month or so. All the while, though, I just couldn't shake the thought of the person who had sold me heroin during my previous trip to Boston. I always felt incomplete and never felt that I had gotten back to normal. I hadn't used in almost three months, but I still felt like something wasn't right. I was cold a lot, I felt empty, depressed, and lonely, and I always knew that one shot of heroin would take all those bad feelings away. That's how powerful my addiction was; even after months without using, I was still addicted. I didn't recognize that I needed treatment and willpower to really break my habit; not just a few months of abstinence. I decided to find my connection in Boston and buy some heroin.

Of course, my life went downhill from there, and before long, I lost my apartment and had to spend some nights sleeping under a bridge. Rather than go back to live on my sister's couch, and faced with the prospect of permanent homelessness, I decided I would go back to detox and that everything would be okay. That lasted about three days, during which I met a kindred spirit who I believed had qualities that could be an asset in acquiring heroin. He'd never been to New York, and I convinced him to come back with me by telling him how much better the drug scene was there than in Boston. Fortunately, as with many of my other drug-using acquaintances, our partnership was short-lived and we went our separate ways after a few weeks. Some time later, I heard people talking about a halfway house in Arizona. It sounded like a nice place, so I convinced my parents to give me two hundred dollars for a bus ticket and the first week's rent. I headed west. As soon as I got there I found a job at a pizza place, then at a little café.

Things went well for a short period. I moved through the house's recovery plan, and I met a nice girl. Then I made the fatal mistake of deciding to start drinking and smoking marijuana again. As you can imagine, soon there was some speculation about my behavior at the halfway house and I was asked to submit to a urinalysis. I declined and moved out. I kept my job, got a nice apartment, and began selling marijuana and other substances to some people I had met.

I flew home to New York for Christmas looking good, with all new clothes and not having used heroin in three months. I had money, and all of my friends and family were proud. Everyone looked at me and thought, "Wow, he's making it, he's doing really well." But I got around some of the old friends, some still using heroin, and it didn't take long for me to join in and pick up where I'd left off.

For a while, I had what you might call a minor habit. It lasted a couple of days, but I made it through. Back in Arizona, I felt pretty much back to normal, and soon thought to myself, "I'm in a place where I don't even know if they have heroin." I'd never even come across anybody who'd done it out there. But I still traveled in circles of people who could put me in touch with others who had access to pretty much any drug imaginable. I happened to be introduced to someone who claimed he could get anything I wanted. I ended up buying from him so-called Mexican Mud, black-tar heroin, and so began my steady decline in Arizona. Within a month, I'd lost everything. I was back to owing people money, having people look for me, stealing from my friends, and losing my apartment. I was homeless again.

Within a month, I'd lost everything.

At this same time, some friends of mine who had decided they had to leave New York came out to Arizona, where I was already using, even sleeping on the streets some nights. Since we were soon forced to turn to theft to support our habits, we decided to leave Arizona before one of us was arrested. I found myself heading farther west.

California was a turning point for me because, up until that time, I had had support from home, I had had resources, no matter how limited or remote. I had kept in touch with my parents. But by the time we reached California, I'd burned all my bridges, severed all my ties to home. I was on my own. I was also still on probation in New York and I hadn't reported to my probation officer, as I was mandated to, in a long time, so I knew that I was in violation of my probation. I'd be arrested if I returned to New York. All of these factors combined as I found myself living a desperate life of crime and drug use in California.

This was Long Beach, and you've already learned about my hellish experience there, living on a filthy rooftop, stealing daily to support my addiction. I ran around with gang members. My friends and I were beat up by the police. We were beat up by the gang members. My ultimate brush with total despair occurred in California. It was the first place I seriously considered suicide, and I lived like I wanted to die. I took stupid risks, thinking that if I lived dangerously enough, I'd eventually end up dead.

After six months of robbing and stealing, running from gangs, and living on rooftops, something inside of me shifted and I decided to go back east. I hadn't stopped using, though, and after a few days of hustling to save up the money to catch a Greyhound to New Jersey, I was on my way with a gram of black tar. I had no money for food or anything else I might need along the way, so by the time I reached Chicago I was sick and looking to buy heroin. I didn't know anyone there or who to contact to get a fix; instead I ended up getting ripped off trying to buy drugs on the street. After nearly missing my bus, I endured another 15 hours of physical and emotional hell on the remainder of the bus ride, sweating, stinking, nauseated, and afraid.

Returning to an Unfamiliar Home

When I finally reached my hometown, no one wanted to see me. They were all afraid of what I had become capable of. I was sleeping in abandoned houses in the town that I grew up in, where my family worked, where I had gone to school. I was a disgrace. My friends' parents hated me because I've given their kids drugs.

One of the major themes of addiction—at least for me—is the concept of escape: escape from responsibilities, family, work, relationships, school, but mainly escape from ourselves. As you've learned from my story so far, it seemed that wherever I ended up I always wanted to be somewhere else. I'd moved to Arizona only to go on to California when the timing seemed right. California

...it seemed that wherever I ended up I always wanted to be somewhere else.

soon proved useless in solving my problems for me, so I returned to New York, thinking that was the answer. A few months after returning to New York, I found myself wanting to go back to California. By now the police were looking for me in New York for violating probation, and the people who knew me in the town where I grew up had grown to despise me. My family and friends were actually beginning to think that my being gone, possibly for good, might not be such a bad thing. I didn't disagree with them. In a cruel twist of irony, I now *did* have something to escape from: the horrible situation in which my drug abuse and desperate behavior had ensnared me.

I had decided to return to California, but I knew I needed a hefty supply of heroin to get me through the long bus ride. The first time I tried to score, I was robbed during the deal, and I ended up trying to buy at a housing project in New Jersey. I spent my last twenty dollars on two bags and fell asleep in the bushes alongside the projects. The idea of returning to California faded away, and for the next three months this was my home. Once again I was hoping for death. Death surrounded me every day and no matter how high I got, the horror of my surroundings always came back. I spent the majority of my days in the stairwells of the projects, quite possibly the vilest places I have ever been. The smell of feces and garbage was overwhelming. Needles and empty crack vials littered the floor.

There are places that exist outside of the life that most respectable, law-abiding people know, places engulfed by darkness and disarray. During these days I watched shootings, stabbings, beatings. I saw junkies stripped of shoes and jackets, dead for days. As a kid, before I'd become an addict, I would never have imagined that this type of reality existed, let alone that I would willingly immerse myself in it. I'd contracted Hepatitis C (a severe viral infection of the liver) from sharing needles. That, plus a steady diet of next to nothing except cheap beers, heroin, and crack, was quickly destroying my liver. I could not keep food down, I could not get up off the curb without help, and I was beginning to jaundice, my eyes and skin turning yellow from poor liver function. If I had stayed on the street for another month I would have died. Using heroin as I did during that time was almost like being dead.

I felt nothing but utter despair. My family believed I had gone back to California. Eventually, I was arrested for shoplifting, and when I called a cousin to ask him to bail me out of jail, he hung up on me and called my parents to tell them where I really was.

At the time, I was experiencing a curious emotional divide within myself. Frequently, I had no feelings, in particular of guilt or remorse. I felt numb, my senses and emotions deadened from having dumped so many deadly chemicals into my body. But then whenever I began to feel sick from withdrawal, I was simply overwhelmed with the shame and despair that had come with years and years of using. Naturally this only made me want more heroin, so I could go back to feeling numb. Feeling nothing certainly seemed more desirable than feeling the grief of a long-term drug addiction.

After my parents bailed me out of jail, I went home with them and then back to detox. I tried rehab, but it was just too difficult and I couldn't commit to it. There were just so many layers of shame, and I'd been using so hard. I was still sick. I begged my mother for two days to lend me her car and she finally just gave in and let me take it. I left rehab and tried to drive back to the projects to buy more heroin. Instead I crashed and totaled the car.

I had driven recklessly, faster than I should have, and gone to turn on a wet corner. I woke up in a twisted, mangled wreck upside down in the middle of the street. People pulled me out and I came to, but was in shock. I was utterly mad; my mind was disorganized with a gripping need for heroin. I was so addled that I actually tried to flip the car back over by myself, thinking that it might be okay. By then an ambulance was pulling up.

"This Is Your Brain on Drugs"

So you can see that, by this time, heroin had taken over my life. In fact, in many ways, it had become my entire life. Getting drugs and using them and then getting them some more was all that I cared about and all that I did. Everything else— my family, my friends, my education, my hopes for my future, any other interests at all— had faded away. The same was true for my sense of honesty, integrity, and self-respect. All that was left was the desperate, insatiable need to get heroin.

Getting drugs and using them and then getting them some more was all that I cared about and all that I did.

But my addiction not only affected my behavior. It also had a very damaging impact on my brain, that all-important organ that makes me who I am. You might recall that TV commercial some years ago, the one with the ominous voiceover saying, "This is your brain on drugs," as an egg sizzles in a frying pan. Well, it's a lot more complicated than that because the human brain is itself incredibly complex. It is a mass of tissue that weighs only about three pounds, but it contains millions of cells that make billions of connections with each other. It is vastly more elaborate than any computer. Drugs of abuse are chemicals that exploit some of the features that make this marvelous system work so well. They distort and subvert how the brain functions and turn processes that evolved over millions of years to help our species survive into processes that can harm us. There are a number of ways drugs are able to do this.

The Blood-Brain Barrier

The bloodstream serves as the body's major transport system, carrying nutrients, oxygen, and components of the immune system; signaling molecules and much more to go where they're needed; and removing what your body doesn't need, like carbon dioxide and wastes. In most parts of the body, the blood vessels have walls that permit all sorts of substances to pass through, going either to or from the surrounding cells.

This is not the case in the brain. The blood-brain barrier is a thin membrane that separates the brain from the bloodstream, and is composed of tightly packed cells that, for the most part, prevent potentially toxic molecules from leaving the blood-stream and entering the brain. It works so well that even many of the medicines we take cannot get from the blood to the brain, and medicines intended to affect the brain specifically must be specially designed to pass through the blood-brain barrier.

Drugs of abuse are effective partly because they defeat this most basic natural defense. They are able to do so because their chemical structures mimic natural molecules that belong in the brain. By mistaking toxic drugs for natural chemicals, the blood-brain barrier can be penetrated, and the brain becomes vulnerable to the mind-altering effects of drugs like cocaine, heroin, nicotine, and others.

The Brain's Reward System

The brain organizes and carries out its many complicated tasks through the principle of specialization. Specialization consists of many separate and distinct brain regions, and the cells of each region are responsible for particular sets of tasks. Different sections are responsible for such functions as planning for the future and exercising judgment (an ability that doesn't fully mature until people reach their mid-twenties, which is why teenagers don't always show the best judgment and sometimes can't predict the long-term consequences of actions such as taking drugs). Other parts of the brain handle other tasks, such as vision and memory.

Scientific study has shown that drug abuse and addiction don't happen in just one area of the brain; instead they are intimately involved with reward-related brain regions that researchers refer to as the *reward circuit*. Rather than one specific structure or area, the reward circuit is a system of chemical processes that has evolved over many millions of years to ensure our survival as a species. The reward circuit ensures that we feel pleasure and avoid pain by engaging in activities essential for survival, such as eating, drinking fluids, sleeping, and procreating. Thanks to the reward circuit, eating when we're hungry, drinking when we're thirsty, sleeping when we're tired, and having sex feel so good and are so satisfying that we want to do them again and again. We humans are said to be "neurologically wired" to repeat experiences that are good for us, because our brains tell us that, for the most part, these experiences are pleasurable.

Drugs like heroin, cocaine, marijuana, and others chemically manipulate this complex system of rewards to trick the brain into thinking that it is engaging in behaviors that are essential to survival. So in the same way that eating feels good when we

...in the same way that eating feels good when we are hungry, drugs can make us feel good, too.

are hungry, drugs can make us feel good, too. The problem is that taking drugs does not actually contribute to our survival as humans; instead, doing so is actually harmful to our health.

What Makes This Trickery Possible?

But that's only part of the story. Drugs like heroin make us feel good the first time we take them—maybe much better than eating when we're hungry or sleeping when we're tired. How? How can a chemical extracted from the seemingly innocent poppy seed have such a powerfully devastating effect on the human brain?

As you can probably imagine, this isn't an easy question to answer. Research is ongoing to learn more about the interactions and processes that take place when a foreign substance fiddles with the brain's delicate chemistry; scientists have made great strides in the past few years with brain imaging techniques and imaginative experiments, but there's still a long way to go. What we do know is that brain chemicals called *neurotransmitters* are an important piece of the puzzle. Neurotransmitters are the brain's chemical messengers, and they transmit, relay, and amplify electrical signals between the brain cells called *neurons* and other cells. Neurons are the basic active cells of the brain and nervous system. They account for all the functions, feelings, and sensations that happen in our thinking and feeling minds. The brain has millions upon millions of neurons. The spaces between the cells are called *synapses*.

A neuron's main job is sending and receiving signals or messages to and from other neurons. The brain carries out its normal functions by exchanging, organizing, and interpreting these messages. Neurons exchange signals and messages by sending out and receiving neurotransmitters in a process a bit like e-mail. Picture two people sitting at computers a mile away from one another. They can send and receive e-mail even though they are not in direct contact; one person can read an e-mail and act according to what the e-mail says, and the other can do the same. In this scenario, the computers are like our neurons, and neurotransmitters are like the e-mail messages themselves—they move between the two computers despite the fact that they are not touching. The space between the computers is the synapse. The process of information transfer in the brain happens at an incredibly high speed, and the physical space between neurons can be measured on a microscopic level.

In the same way that e-mail messages are sent into cyberspace by computers, neurons send signals to other neurons by releasing neurotransmitters into synapses where other neurons can pick them up and receive and interpret the messages they carry. Once the neurotransmitter has completed its job, it is absorbed back into the neuron in a process called *reuptake*. (Picture saving that received e-mail in a folder, since one of our computer users might want to send it again someday.)

Here is where the story gets a little more complicated. Each neuron is equipped to receive specific types of neurotransmitters. This is possible because each type of neurotransmitter molecule has a unique shape. Proteins called *receptors* cover the neuron's surface, and they function as tiny molecular locks. Each of the receptors has a particular shape of its own that matches the specific shape of a certain neurotransmitter. Just as you can unlock the front door of your house with a key that has exactly the right shape, a neurotransmitter or other chemical that has exactly the right shape can fit into and bind to a matching receptor. Different receptors in the brain serve different functions, and drugs of abuse manipulate these functions.

When a molecule (and it doesn't have to be a neurotransmitter, as we'll see in a moment) binds to a receptor, the neuron responds in some way. Some molecules stimulate the neuron to emit its own neurotransmitters. Others prevent the neuron from emitting its own neurotransmitters; these chemicals are called *inhibitory*.

Drugs of Abuse Are Chemical Copycats

Quite by accident, this elegant system of neurotransmitters and receptors provides the route for drugs to infiltrate our brains and cause addiction. By pure chance, substances in certain plants also have chemical shapes that fit into some of the same brain receptor "locks" as our own homemade neurotransmitters. It's as if some stranger just happened to have a key exactly like the one that opens your front door. So, just as that stranger could rob your house using his copy of the key, these plant molecules can bind to the receptors of cells in your brain that usually serve quite different purposes. Combine this with the fact that some of the chemicals in drugs allow them to sneak across the blood-brain barrier, and drugs become even more harmful to the human brain.

Drugs act as chemical impostors because their molecular structure is so similar to some of the molecules found naturally in the brain. Once they cross the blood-brain barrier, drugs of abuse trigger the reward circuit, causing us to feel pleasure. Each drug appears to stimulate the

> Drugs act as chemical impostors because their molecular structure is so similar to some of the molecules found naturally in the brain.

reward circuit in a different way, and researchers continue to investigate exactly how drugs of abuse behave in the brain. What's more, drugs activate our desire to repeat this pleasurable experience, tricking our brains into thinking we're engaging in repetitive behavior that is essential to our survival. But instead of encouraging us to repeat an activity that relates to survival, such as eating or sleeping, these copycat substances simply encourage us to consume more of the same substance.

An example of a copycat substance known since ancient times is opium, which comes from the seeds of bright red flowers known as poppies. Modern drugs such as codeine, morphine, and heroin are made by extracting chemicals from the poppy's seeds (or by synthetically creating similar compounds in a lab). These chemicals are known as *opioids,* and they bind to the receptors usually used by natural brain chemicals called *endorphins* and *encephalins,* which are involved in relieving pain, among a number of other important functions. Endorphins are associated with feelings of satisfaction, and they are known to turn off unpleasant feelings within the brain. They're known as the brain's own opiates (*opiate* is the term for the chemical extracted from the poppy seed), and any drug that mimics the endorphins' action within the brain will likely also produce feelings of satisfaction and block unpleasant sensations. This is why taking heroin or codeine makes us feel good. Morphine has long been considered one of the very best drugs for relieving severe pain and is widely used in medicine. Another chemical impostor is tetrahydrocannabinol (THC), the active chemical in marijuana, which fits into the receptor used by the natural brain chemical *anandamide.* This produces in most people a mild, short period of intoxication and a feeling of euphoria.

Locking onto receptors and triggering some of the brain's own reward mechanisms isn't the only way drugs mess with our minds. They also disrupt the normal movement of neuro-transmitters and change the ways neurons act. Changes to the neurons mean changes to the brain. Some drugs can cause more of a neurotransmitter to be released unnecessarily. Al-cohol, heroin, and nicotine, for example, have this effect on the neurotransmitter *dopamine.* Other drugs can block the reuptake of a neurotransmitter, causing more of it to remain in the synapses, which wreaks havoc on brain chemistry. Cocaine and amphetamines have this effect. Some drugs can prevent neurotransmitters from binding to their receptors, short-circuiting their action and preventing them from effectively relaying messages. Returning to the e-mail analogy, picture thousands upon thousands of e-mails going to the wrong re-cipients; or one e-mail being sent out hundreds of times in-stead of just once; or e-mails not being received by the correct recipient even though the address is correct. Pretty soon all communication between computers would devolve into a mess of misinterpreted messages and nonsense. This is what can happen to the brain when it's been hijacked by drugs.

Dosage and Method of Administration

Exactly how effectively a drug disrupts normal brain function also depends on two additional factors: how much of the drug is consumed and how it is administered. For a drug to be effective, it must be concentrated within the body above a certain amount (for example, the *blood alcohol content* (BAC) is used by law enforcement officers to measure the level of al-cohol in the blood; it directly correlates to how intoxicated a person is). But no one can consume an unlimited amount of any toxic chemical without the risk of overdose, which can often be fatal. Too much heroin, for instance, can cause an effect known as *respiratory depression,* during which the user stops breathing. Respiratory depression is one of the ways that heroin overdoses can be fatal. Generally, the more one smokes, drinks, inhales, or shoots, the more severe the impairment.

The route by which a drug enters the body also influences its effect upon the brain. Some methods of administration work faster than others, and some allow more of the drug to get to the brain. Smoking drugs is the fastest way to get high, since the drug reaches the brain in seconds. Smoked drugs like marijuana, crack-cocaine, and nicotine pass straight from the lungs and into the bloodstream, and then are pumped to the brain by the heart. Injecting into a vein allows the drug to reach the brain nearly as quickly because it reaches the bloodstream almost immediately as well, but the chemical takes a longer route to the brain. A snorted or sniffed drug takes longer still to reach the brain because it has to pass through the nose's mucous lining before it reaches the bloodstream. Injecting into a muscle is considerably slower. Drugs taken by mouth are slowest of all because they have to pass through the stomach or into the intestine before they can be absorbed into the blood and carried to the brain.

Tolerance

But how do drugs that initially start out causing pleasant feelings gain such a hold that people will do anything to take them and ignore the terrible problems they bring? Why avoid using drugs if they induce such pleasant sensations? One reason is the terrible, intense craving that they can cause; the need to satisfy these cravings immediately can overpower our reason, causing us to steal or lie—when ordinarily we'd do no such thing—in order to obtain drugs. Another is a concept I've mentioned a few times already: tolerance.

A key concept in addiction science, tolerance occurs when an addict must constantly increase the dose of his or her drug

A drug user can begin to develop tolerance on the first occasion of drug use, and the increase in dose as the addiction progresses can be staggering.

of choice in order to obtain the same effect that was once achieved with much smaller doses. A drug user can begin to develop tolerance on the first occasion of drug use, and the increase in dose as the addiction progresses can be staggering. For instance, heroin addicts have been known to use doses one hundred times stronger than when they first began using, just to achieve the same high. As an addict's dose goes up and up and up, the risks of overdose increase as well, as does the desperation with which the addict will seek drugs.

This happens because the brain, along with most biological systems, is programmed to restore itself to its original state when manipulated—in this case, the enormous surges of neurotransmitters that drugs cause. In an attempt to compensate for the heavy dopamine release that the drugs cause, for instance, the brain itself cuts production of the neurotransmitter. It also slashes the number of neuron receptors available to respond to dopamine. When the natural balance of brain chemicals is upset by an external substance, such as cocaine or heroin, the brain works hard to neutralize the effect of the drug—by flooding the brain with new chemicals, by reducing the sensitivity to receptors, and so on. So the drug addict who continues to increase his or her dosage is fighting a pitched battle with the brain, which is fighting desperately to adapt to the rapidly changing levels of chemicals.

This means that when the drug is *not* present, the addict's normal ability to feel pleasure is drastically reduced because the brain has cut back so dramatically on pleasure-related chemical production. Without the drugs, the brain's reward system no longer functions properly. Life now seems gray, flat, and dismal, and the addict feels irritable and depressed. Even the things that he or she used to love doing don't feel good any more. The brain is no longer rewarding the addict for positive, survival-oriented behavior like eating. So to get rid of these terrible feelings, the addict needs more of the drug that caused this problem in the first place. Unfortunately, now much more of the drug is needed to obtain that same old feeling of pleasure, the high or the rush that once came so easily.

Withdrawal

Addictive drug use often leads to an unpleasant series of symptoms if drug use ceases suddenly. I've mentioned this phenomenon several times already and have experienced it myself: withdrawal. It may be related to the chemical imbalance left behind when drug use is halted. For example, opioids like heroin and codeine suppress the activity of *noradrenaline,* a neurotransmitter involved with alertness and arousal. Over time the brain becomes accustomed to this suppression, but when the opioid abuse ends, noradrenaline levels soar and the drug user experiences high levels of hyperactivity. This is because there is now too much noradrenaline in the system. It takes a while for the brain to get back to normal.

The symptoms of withdrawal can be psychological, such as depression, anxiety, panic attacks, lethargy, or paranoia, or they can be physical, such as severe body pains, twitches, seizures, nausea, diarrhea, yawning, fatigue, or sleeplessness. The symptoms can vary in onset, duration, and intensity from individual to individual, and from drug to drug. While withdrawal is always an unpleasant experience, withdrawal from alcohol, sedatives, and barbiturates can be lethal and should be overseen by medical professionals.

Because these symptoms are so unpleasant, addicts will use a drug as much to avoid withdrawal as to experience the pleasurable feelings that first led them to take the drug.

The Long-Term Effects on the Brain of Chronic Drug Use

The brain is a remarkable but delicate organ; it can't be subjected to repeated drug use without incurring some damage. Until recently, it was impossible for scientists to really see just how dramatically and negatively substance abuse can affect the brain—they didn't have tools that were sophisticated enough for the job, and had to rely on observing how people behaved to measure brain damage. Today, however, new understanding of brain chemistry, along with sophisticated imaging techniques, such as magnetic resonance imaging (MRI) and positron emission tomography (PET), have allowed scientists to gain access to the brain in order to better understand how it is affected by things like injury, mental illness, and drug abuse.

The results are startling. We need no longer rely on anecdotal evidence to ascertain how chemicals can harm the brain. For instance, a study conducted at the University of Edinburgh and published in 2005 found that young people who abused heroin and other opiates had actually sustained the kind of brain damage most often seen in older people with Alzheimer's disease. The study suggests that opiate abuse prematurely ages young brains by causing severe nerve cell damage and cell death within the brain. Some heavy heroin users have been rendered comatose, with large lesions on their brains. Similarly, methamphetamine use has been shown to cause damage to blood vessels and nerve endings in the brain, and to cause harmful changes in brain chemicals. As a result, young methamphetamine users are at higher risk for cognitive impairment, and for developing movement disorders such as Parkinson's disease that are ordinarily seen in much older people.

Lest you think that long-term brain damage is only a risk for users of hardcore drugs like methamphetamine and heroin, know that alcohol and marijuana abuse pose some of the same kinds of risks. Consuming large quantities of alcohol in a short period of time (binge drinking), for instance, has been shown by Duke University researchers to cause brain damage in young rats and to cause memory loss later in life—even after these drinking patterns have ceased. Parallel research on human adolescent drinkers is currently under way. Likewise, studies have shown that long-term use of marijuana can impair performance on tests even when the user isn't high at the time of the test, because marijuana remains in the fat stores of the body long after the user has smoked.

Scientists know all these things now thanks to new techniques that allow them to see the physical effects on the brain of substance abuse. Single photon emission computed tomography (SPECT), MRI, and PET scans produce images of the brain on a computer screen that show dark spots or lesions where brain damage has occurred; electroencephalography (EEG) measures the electrical activity of the brain. Damage due to substance abuse most often occurs in the areas of the brain associated with memory, learning, and emotional well-being.

The good news is that a lot of these effects may be reversible if the assault of drug abuse on the brain ends, but scientists still don't know just how completely the brain can repair itself. That's just one reason why it's important for you to get clean now—the

Damage due to substance abuse most often occurs in the areas of the brain associated with memory, learning, and emotional well-being.

longer the duration of abuse and the older your brain becomes without having a chance to heal, the more likely you are to have to live with the effects of brain damage permanently.

Brain Damage 3-D

Even though I can explain to you the negative consequences of taking drugs, I can't show you a picture of these consequences. Lynn Marie Smith, however, had a chance to see what her chronic drug abuse had done to her brain, and she describes that experience in her book *Rolling Away:*

The nurse took a seat at the computer and began punching away at the keys. "First, Sherry is going to pull up the scan of a normal person," he said, pointing with his pen at the screen.

A normal person... give me a break.

A few seconds passed before a green 3D image of a brain appeared on the large monitor. "Now you can see here that this one is plump and full... and now we're going to pull up the image of your brain next to it."

Drum roll, please...

I blinked and there it was. My stomach fell to the floor. I heard my mother quietly gasp in my right ear. I couldn't take my eyes off the screen.

"As you can see here, Lynn, all of these dark areas—Sherry, will you please rotate the image," he said.

I watched my brain move in a circle around the screen. I could see right through it. Pieces were missing. Swiss cheese came to mind. That couldn't be good. No... no... no.

Pointing to the screen with his pen. "Your brain looks like a cobweb, almost moth eaten. These dark spots are areas of inactivity, they look like holes, but they're not. These are areas of inactivity, lack of blood flow. Memory, decision making, mood, depth perception, all of these things are affected. Lynn, how old are you? Eighteen? Twenty?" he asked.

"Twenty-two," I said.

"Looking at your brain image, I would say that this was a sixty, sixty-five-year-old woman who has had multiple strokes..." (Reprinted from Lynn Marie Smith, *Rolling Away: My Agony with Ecstasy* [New York: Atria Books, 2005].)

Different Types of Drugs of Abuse

There are of course many ways to get high, and from my story alone, you've already heard about a number of them. You may be intimately acquainted with one or more of them yourself. Now let's look more closely at them—indeed, at all the drugs most commonly used by young people, as well as the means by which the substances are used, how they act on the brain, and what risks they pose.

Alcohol

I mentioned earlier that alcohol is the most widely used psychoactive substance among adolescents. Beer is the most preferred form of alcohol, but a variety of sweet, fruit-flavored drinks are growing in popularity. It has been reported that, by senior year, eight out of ten high school students have used alcohol to some degree, and according to the National Institute on Alcohol Abuse and Alcoholism (NIAAA), underage use of alcohol is more likely to kill young people than all other illegal drugs combined. This is primarily due to car accidents, but also contributing to this disturbing statistic are the many alcohol poisonings, homicides, and suicides that occur when young people are intoxicated.

Statistics on adolescent abuse of and addiction to alcohol are scarce, but one study showed that 0.4% to 9.6% of young people abuse alcohol (meaning they exhibit problematic behavior associated with drinking), while 0.6% to 4.3% may be addicted to alcohol. By definition, any adolescent use of alcohol is considered abuse, since it's illegal for anyone under the age of 21 to drink. For adults to meet a diagnosis of alcohol abuse, according to the *Diagnostic and Statistical Manual of Mental Disorders,* fourth edition (or *DSM-IV,* the manual of diagnoses of the mental health world), they must meet one of these four criteria: Their use (1) is recurrent, causing serious consequences; (2) is physically dangerous; (3) causes legal problems; or (4) results in persistent social or interpersonal problems. There is some debate among experts whether these criteria should apply to adolescent alcohol abuse as well.

Alcohol is a powerful sedative that acts on the brain, affects behavior and perception, and can cause dependence or addiction. Many people find alcohol use to be relaxing, anxiety reducing, and even euphoric. It relieves inhibitions and can sometimes make drinkers feel invincible. But overuse of alcohol can lead to nausea, vomiting, confusion, depression, and even death. Adolescents may lose control of their drinking by consuming more alcohol over a given period of time than they intended. Repeated drinking can lead to tolerance—one of the most reported symptoms of alcohol dependence in adolescents—and withdrawal symptoms if alcohol consumption ends suddenly. Severe withdrawal symptoms are almost never seen in adolescents, but include physiological effects such as delirium tremens (DT), in which a drinker experiences confusion, agitation, hallucinations, and psychosis.

For a diagnosis of alcohol *dependence,* a person must meet three of seven criteria in the *DSM-IV:* (1) withdrawal; (2) tolerance; (3) larger amounts consumed than intended; (4) unsuccessful attempts to stop; (5) excessive time spent drinking; (6) important activities given up; and (7) continued use despite awareness of negative effects of drinking. Again, expert opinion differs as to whether these criteria can be applied to adolescents. Research is ongoing into this question. The important take-home message here, though, is that any of these symptoms, alone or combined, should indicate to any underage drinker that there is a problem, and that it might be time to seek help.

Alcohol affects females more dramatically than males for two reasons. Once into adolescence, females on average weigh less and are smaller than males, but they are increasingly encouraged to match their male drinking partners ounce for ounce. Because their bodies are not as large, however, they are therefore more vulnerable to intoxication. As well, females have less of the liver enzyme *dehydrogenase,* which metabolizes alcohol. More of what is consumed therefore reaches the female bloodstream.

Going on a Bender

Adults usually drink to relax or socialize, but adolescents often drink to get drunk. This type of alcohol abuse is known as *binge drinking.* It's extremely dangerous and can lead to fatal and near-fatal automobile accidents, date rape, aggressive fights, and unprotected sex leading to pregnancy and sexually transmitted diseases. It can also lead to alcohol poisoning: Vomiting, loss of consciousness, cold or clammy skin, and irregular breathing can indicate an alcohol overdose, and in severe cases the brain can shut down and basic bodily functions such as breathing can cease. Suicide is much more common in those who are intoxicated, as alcohol can lower inhibitions and worsen depression.

Five or more drinks for a guy and four or more for a girl on a single occasion is considered an alcohol binge. Statistics from the Harvard School of Public Health show that close to half of college students—both men and women—engaged in this dangerous form of alcohol abuse in a two-week period. Surveys also show that a quarter of high school freshman and more than a third of high school seniors have done so. Students who binge in high school are even more likely to binge when they get to college. Even students who don't binge reported being affected by it, by having their sleep or studying disturbed, having to take care of a drunken fellow student, having to fight off unwelcome sexual advances, having their property damaged, or arguing with or having been assaulted by a student who was drunk.

Cannabis

Weed, pot, chronic, herb, ganja—whatever slang terms are used for it, marijuana is made from a plant called *Cannabis sativa.* Next to alcohol, it's the most commonly used illegal drug among adolescents, and it can be used in more than one form. The dried plant can be ground up into small pieces and smoked, either in hand-rolled cigarettes (joints), in pipes, or in cigars (blunts). When users smoke marijuana the effect is almost immediate, and the substance reaches the brain within seconds of the first puff. Marijuana can also be cooked into baked goods, which, when eaten, produce a high after as long as an hour. A gummy substance called a resin can also be taken from the plant and formed into cubes or balls, then broken into pieces and swallowed or smoked in pipes. This is called hashish or hash.

Cannabis contains a chemical called tetrahydrocannabinol (THC) that causes euphoria and relaxation. When THC reaches the brain, its chemical copycat nature allows it to easily lock onto cells using the body's natural cannabinoid receptors, which are particularly plentiful in several parts of the brain: the *cerebellum,* which is a region involved in coordinating the body's movements; the *hippocampus,* crucial for memory and learning; the *cerebral cortex,* vital for higher intellectual and cognitive functions; and the *nucleus acubens,* which is associated with feelings of reward. What all this means is that marijuana impairs our ability to control bodily movements, to learn and remember things, to tackle complex

... marijuana impairs our ability to control bodily movements, to learn and remember things, to tackle complex problems and ideas, and to make sound judgments.

problems and ideas, and to make sound judgments. It has sedative, mildly hallucinogenic, anxiolytic (anxiety-reducing), and both appetite-suppressing and appetite-stimulating properties. After the euphoria passes, some people experience depression or anxiety.

People who are high on marijuana are much more prone to accidents caused by bad judgment, clumsy movements, and inattention to dangers and changing circumstances. Studies have shown that, after first having been tested for alcohol, between 6 and 11% of people who die in accidents had THC in their systems at the time of their deaths. When the National Highway Traffic Safety Administration tested the effect of marijuana on driving ability, it found that people were slower to react, less alert, and less able to react quickly and correctly. It has been suggested that cannabis may also negatively affect the immune system, rendering the body more vulnerable to disease and infection.

Substantial use of marijuana can also damage memory—both the ability to remember new things and the ability to retrieve memories already formed—and attention, especially the ability to shift attention among different focuses. This can, of course, really affect school work and the ability to concentrate in sports or on the job. Some people who have taken very large doses suffer psychosis, which is an acute and severe symptom that includes hallucinations (seeing or hearing things that are not there) or delusions (believing things that are not true). Using marijuana can also make it more difficult to stop smoking tobacco, research shows; on the flipside, teens who smoke cigarettes are much more likely to also smoke pot. Suicide and suicidal ideation are more common among users of marijuana, and as with any form of smoking, heavy use can damage the heart and lungs.

Many people believe that marijuana is not addictive, but in fact it can lead to addiction in some individuals. These people use the drug compulsively and develop tolerance to it very quickly, leading the user to need larger and more frequent doses to get high. When use of the drug stops, addicted users suffer withdrawal symptoms that include cravings, anxiety, irritability, nausea, and sleep problems.

Hallucinogens

Hallucinogens cause profound distortions in sensory perception accompanied by a relatively high level of consciousness. Despite the name of this class of drugs, hallucinations themselves are uncommon; instead, the user experiences an alteration of visual images, sounds, and physical sensations. Mood swings and feeling out of control are also common in hallucinogen use.

Plant-based hallucinogens such as mescaline, psilocybin mushrooms, and peyote have been used by people for thousands of years; these chemicals are similar to some of those found in the brain, such as *serotonin, dopamine*, and *norepinephrine*. The hallucinogenic drug most commonly used among adolescents today is LSD (lysergic acid diethylamide). During the early twentieth century, LSD was first synthesized in laboratories from chemicals present in a fungus. It is distributed in a variety of forms, most often in quarter-inch squares of paper saturated with the drug, or in pills.

Swallowing a tiny amount can induce an "acid trip" that may range from pleasant to horrifying. The perception of sounds, colors, and smells is distorted, and objects and even the body itself can seem to change shape. Time may seem to slow down. Sometimes people feel that their minds are extra sharp and intelligent and that their thoughts are brilliantly creative or leading to deep spiritual insights. At other times, people experience nightmarish trips full of terror and anxiety. LSD can cause difficulty in recognizing reality, communicating with other people, and thinking rationally. In rarer cases, psychosis, mood swings, depression, and mania can result from its use. The effects of heavy LSD use can be psychologically traumatic, and a typical trip can last anywhere from 6 to 12 hours. On occasion the person may suffer the effects for years after actually using the drug. LSD users may also experience what are known as *flashbacks*—for example, they see bright colors or flashes—even when they have not used the drug in many years.

LSD can cause difficulty in recognizing reality, communicating with other people, and thinking rationally.

Scientists believe that the drug acts by affecting the receptors that bind to the neurotransmitter *serotonin,* especially in a part of the brain called the *cerebral cortex,* which affects our moods and our abilities to perceive and to know. It also causes disruption in a part of the brain called the *locus coeruleus,* which processes sensory information from many parts of the body.

Phencyclidine and Ketamine

Phencyclidine (PCP, angel dust) and ketamine (K, special K, vitamin K, kat valium) cause a feeling of detachment or dissociation from reality, but not hallucinations. PCP, the most commonly used drug in this class, was developed for use as an anesthetic in surgical operations. It is no longer considered safe for use in humans because it can cause severe delirium and agitation. Veterinarians have, however, used it during operations on animals.

Both of these drugs can be taken in pill form or as a powder, and they can be smoked or injected. Their usual effects—a trance-like or out-of-body state—are hard to predict, and some users become violent or suicidal. Panic and fear are other possible effects. Both are considered addictive because tolerance and dependence can develop over an extended period of use. Overdose can result in delirium, psychosis, seizures, and coma. Some people have been known to use ketamine, which is tasteless and odorless, to surreptitiously drug others (by, say, slipping it into their drinks) in order to victimize them, as in date rape and sexual assaults.

Phencyclidine and ketamine both alter the distribution of the important neurotransmitter *glutamate,* which is involved in pain, in thinking, learning and remembering, and in emotion. They also affect receptors for the neurotransmitter dopamine, which is involved in creating the rush, or euphoric feelings, caused by a number of drugs of abuse.

Opiates

Opiate drugs include opium, heroin, morphine, codeine and oxycodone. While only opium is a natural plant product that comes from the seed pods of the poppy flower, the others are drugs synthesized in the laboratory to have actions similar or stronger than the natural product. For thousands of years, people have recognized opium for its ability to block pain. Today, doctors consider morphine one of the strongest pain-killers available, and it is widely used to ease the suffering of people in great pain from severe injuries or diseases such as terminal cancer. Doctors also prescribe oxycodone and codeine for pain from surgery and injuries. All of these are controlled substances, meaning that they are strictly regulated by law and are only available by prescription. Heroin cannot be used legally in the United States.

All of the opiate drugs are addictive and all of them are used as drugs of abuse. Heroin is extremely addictive, as my experience with it shows; it's the most often abused opiate and the fastest acting of the group. Usually sold as a powder, but sometimes as a tar-like substance, it can be injected with a needle, snorted through the nose, or smoked in a pipe.

In the region of the brain related to emotion, heroin causes feelings of pleasure and a temporary rush. Cognition and judgment become cloudy. After that, the user often nods off for a few hours. Users enjoy the intoxication from heroin so much that they become obsessed with it, but tolerance develops rapidly. They can increase their dose 100-fold in an attempt to achieve the same high as was once obtained with lower doses.

Opiates easily pass through the blood-brain barrier. They then lock on to and activate the brain's own opioid receptors, which densely populate reward-related brain regions. This triggers the brain's natural reward system, leading to the feelings of pleasure and satiety (satisfaction). The drug, meanwhile, is also acting on the brain stem, which controls such body processes as breathing—with sometimes fatal results if the individual has taken too large a dose. Respiratory depression, where the user stops breathing, is especially likely to happen with heroin.

About 22% of first-time heroin users become addicted; the drug's addictiveness comes from the intense euphoria that it induces, as well as the intense cravings that come with sustained use. You already know the array of possible results from this addiction: deterioration in daily function

About 22% of first-time heroin users become addicted . . .

and relationships, crime, and for some, the risk of infection with Hepatitis C and HIV/AIDS when they share needles.

Risks of the Needle: HIV/AIDS and Hepatitis C

Certain blood-borne diseases can spread through intravenous drug use when addicts share dirty hypodermic needles.

- HIV/AIDS
  Human Immunodeficiency Virus (HIV), a retrovirus that leads eventually to acquired immune deficiency syndrome, or AIDS, is a condition in which the immune system begins to fail, leading to life-threatening infections. There is no known cure for either of these diseases, and the World Health Organization estimates that AIDS has killed over 25 million people since its discovery in the early 1980s.
- Hepatitis C
  Hepatitis C is a serious viral infection that causes inflammation of the liver. There are often no discernible symptoms of this infection, but if left untreated Hepatitis C can lead to cirrhosis (scarring of the liver) and liver cancer. The illness can be eradicated in some but not all people and results in an estimated 10 to 20 thousand deaths per year in the United States.

Many communities across the country have set up needle exchange programs to help prevent the spread of these infections through intravenous drug use. Such programs inspire a lot of controversy; critics say that their existence condones and promotes drug abuse, while supporters claim that supplying clean needles to the drug-using community decreases transmission of these diseases without increasing rates of intravenous drug use. For more information visit www.nasenorg.

Withdrawal from heroin can be excruciating; it usually sets in within about 8–12 hours of abstinence and lasts from 3 to 5 days. Panic, irritability, depression, cravings, and nausea are among the psychological and physical symptoms of withdrawal.

Cocaine and Other Stimulants

Cocaine, methamphetamine, amphetamine, and dextroamphetamine are known as *stimulants.* They produce a feeling of well-being, increased endurance and energy, euphoria, and a reduced appetite. Cocaine is by far the most abused of this class of drugs; it is extracted from the leaf of a plant called coca and for many years was the active ingredient in certain wines and in Coca-Cola. It is also a powerful pain reliever, and a nonaddictive form of this drug, Novocaine, is still used by dentists.

Cocaine itself has two different chemical versions. One form, cocaine hydrochloride, dissolves in water. Therefore, it can be injected into a vein or sniffed as a powder into the nose, where the body's own mucous dissolves it. Freebase cocaine, also called *crack,* does not dissolve. Sold in large chunks, or rocks, it is easy to smoke in a pipe. Taken this way, the drug races to the brain in seconds. Cocaine heightens sensory perception, making sensations feel more intense, and gives people a feeling of grandiosity—thoughts that they are brilliant and all-powerful. These feelings last only a short time before a user crashes, then wants more. With continued use, thought processes become more and more irrational, and behavior becomes more and more wild and out of control. Because people who are high on cocaine think that they are magically powerful, they often take very dangerous risks that they wouldn't otherwise take. Cocaine can cause an erratic heartbeat, sometimes leading to cardiac arrest or a stroke. After people stop taking the drug, they experience withdrawal symptoms, feeling depressed, anxious, and suspicious, sometimes to extreme degrees. Afterward they often feel very bored and experience strong cravings for cocaine. Withdrawal symptoms, known as a "crash," also include increased appetite, low energy, and reduced sex drive.

Like most drugs of abuse, cocaine activates the brain's pleasure centers, locking onto structures in the reward circuit called *dopamine transporters*. Initially scientists thought that the effect involved dopamine alone, but research has shown that serotonin is probably involved as well. It is highly addictive, particularly in adolescents; about 6% of adolescents become addicted to it within the first year after having tried it. Crack-cocaine is thought to be especially attractive to young people who are already used to smoking cigarettes and marijuana. It is a chunk of commercially made cocaine alkaloid, which, when heated, produces vapors that can be inhaled. This method is known to be even more hazardous than snorting cocaine.

Other drugs in the amphetamine class, such as methamphetamine, are also powerful stimulants. Amphetamine is an artificial chemical that prevents dopamine from being reabsorbed from the synapses of the reward circuit; it also causes the neurons to release more. This activates the brain's reward circuit. Like cocaine, amphetamines produce an intense rush and very strong cravings. Methamphetamine, though similar in many ways to amphetamine, lingers in the brain for far longer; it takes up to twelve times as long to leave the body as cocaine.

Stimulants such as cocaine and amphetamine can induce long-term changes in the brain, such as a drop in the number of dopamine receptors. This may cause feelings of depression when users are not using. Over time, methamphetamine use can lead to severe mental disturbances including hallucinations and mood swings, along with violent behavior.

Inhalants and Volatile Solvents

A huge array of chemicals in common use can produce gases and vapors that can affect the functioning of the brain. Many of these are easily available at home or in stores—glues, paint thinners, cleaning fluids, even gasoline and the fluid in felt-tipped pens. Others come in spray cans of household products like deodorant, paint, insecticide, or hair spray. Sniffing or inhaling these substances is actually more common among children and young adolescents than among older people; one study reported that 6% of kids had tried inhalants on at least one occasion by the fourth grade. Inhalants are often the first experience with harmful drug use that many young people have.

Inhalants are often the first experience with harmful drug use that many young people have.

Breathing in fumes and vapors allows them to reach the brain rapidly, where they can cause a high or a feeling of intoxication or light-headedness. Movements slow, and speech becomes slurred; the ability to walk becomes impaired. The pleasurable effects of using inhalants dissipate almost immediately after inhalation ceases.

Inhalants are not without their own set of withdrawal symptoms, which can include headache and nausea. It's possible to overdose on inhalants if the user passes out while still breathing in fumes or vapor, and such overdoses can be fatal. With repeated use, inhalants can cause loss of consciousness and coma. In the long term, inhalant abuse can cause problems with memory and permanent brain damage. Aside from the brain, the chemicals inhaled move through the liver, kidneys, and nerves, and can cause significant damage to these organs. Some inhalants, such as Freon, are extremely cold, and inhaling them can cause death due to freezing of the lungs.

Club Drugs

Though this is a very diverse group of substances, they're often referred to in a group as *club drugs* because of their popularity at parties and nightclubs. Ketamine (discussed earlier), GHB (Gammahydroxybutyrate), and ecstasy (MDMA) are the three most used club drugs. These substances are thought by many users to be safe, but this is not the case. Many club drugs constitute a rather mixed bag of different chemicals, all of them made in illegal labs. That means there is no way of knowing exactly what chemicals they contain or how strong they are. Overdoses on club drugs can be and have been fatal.

Ecstasy, which has the scientific name *3,4-methylenedioxymethamphetamine,* or *MDMA,* is distributed usually as a pill, and is a stimulant with hallucinogenic properties. It binds to serotonin transporters, causing neurons to release sertotonin, dopamine, and norephinephrine. It is usually taken orally and produces feelings of energy, an altered sense of time, and an enhanced perception of sensory experiences. It may also cause less pleasant effects such as anxiety and agitation, and can impair memory and information processing. Some users have reported withdrawal symptoms, too, which include depression and difficulty concentrating, that can last for many days. Overdose on ecstasy isn't common, but it can be fatal; at high doses, loss of consciousness can occur as a result of hyperthermia (where the body becomes overheated) and dehydration, indicating that the body's ability to regulate temperature has failed. This can bring on multiple organ failure and death.

Many studies on animals have proven that ecstasy can do long-lasting damage to the neurons that contain serotonin. In humans, studies show that ecstasy users suffer confusion, depression, and other effects that impair their ability to function. The drug can also cause dangerous physical symptoms and damage to the liver, kidney, and heart.

Gammahydroxybutyrate, or GHB, is a powerful depressant that causes euphoria, relaxation, and a feeling of being uninhibited. It is a clear, salty liquid that is also used as a date-rape drug. It can cause nausea, vomiting, respiratory depression, and seizures when overdose occurs. Deaths from GHB usually happen when it is used along with alcohol, which is another depressant. It's likely that repeated use leads to tolerance, since users have reported that they must up their dosage to continue getting the same effects. Withdrawal has also been observed, with symptoms including anxiety, delirium, and sleep problems. The combination of tolerance and withdrawal seen with GHB use means it is most likely addictive.

Prescription Drugs

Often times the substances of abuse that young people have the easiest access to can be found within their own medicine cabinets: prescription medications. The three most commonly abused groups of prescription drugs are opioids like oxycodone that are prescribed to treat pain, depressants like Xanax that treat anxiety and sleep disorders, and stimulants, which are often prescribed to treat narcolepsy and attention-deficit disorder.

Prescription opioids include morphine, OxyContin, and codeine, and are highly addictive. When taken improperly, they can cause euphoria by affecting certain pleasure-related regions of the brain. This effect can be enhanced by smoking or injecting the drug, instead of swallowing it in pill form. Physical dependence and addiction are risks of opioid abuse and symptoms like restlessness, muscle and bone pain, diarrhea, and vomiting can accompany withdrawal from these drugs. Overdose on prescription opioids can be fatal if respiratory depression occurs.

Depressants, sometimes referred to as sedatives or tranquilizers, include barbiturates like mephobarbital, and benzodiazepines like Valium and Xanax. They work by slowing down brain function, which makes them especially useful for treating anxiety. Tolerance can develop if these drugs are abused long term, and continued use can lead to physical dependence and possible withdrawal symptoms. Abrupt discontinuation of stimulant abuse can cause seizures because the brain is suddenly jolted out of its slowed-down state and races out of control. Withdrawal from prolonged use of some depressants can be life threatening, and should be done under the supervision of a doctor.

Stimulants like dextroamphetamine and methylphenidate (also known as Ritalin) increase attention, alertness, and energy, and elevate blood pressure and heart rate. They are associated with a release of dopamine in the brain, which can cause feelings of euphoria. As with the other prescription drugs in this section, continued stimulant abuse can lead to physical dependence and addiction. In the short term, use of stimulants by some people can cause feelings of paranoia and hostility. If too much of a stimulant is ingested, irregular heart beat and elevated body temperature may increase the risk for cardiovascular failure (heart attack) or fatal seizures.

One study in 2003 suggested that 4% of young people aged 12 to 17 had used prescription drugs improperly in the past month, while 6% of people 18 to 25 abused these drugs. In some cases, drugs prescribed for psychiatric conditions were more likely to be misused by young people than marijuana. Some data has shown that young women are more likely to abuse prescription drugs than young men, and kids who use other drugs like marijuana and cocaine are more likely to also abuse prescription medications.

> ...4% of young people aged 12 to 17 have used prescription drugs improperly in the past month ...

Cigarettes

It may seem strange to see cigarettes on this list because smoking is such an accepted activity among all sorts of people in the United States. Cigarette smoking by people under the age of 18 (which is illegal) represents the most common form of substance abuse in adolescents. Almost 800,000 people under 18 will become regular smokers each year, and about 90% of smokers began smoking before they were 21.

Smoking during childhood and adolescence can lead to chronic coughing, increased risk for respiratory illness, lowered physical fitness, and a stunting of lung growth. Young people who smoke may have just as hard a time quitting as adults, and most adolescents who've smoked at least 100 cigarettes in their lives, when asked, say they'd like to quit smoking but can't. In fact, there is evidence that the earlier one starts smoking, the harder it is to quit, and the more likely a person is to die of a smoking-related illness. About 440,000 people in the United States die each year from diseases caused by cigarette smoking. These include heart disease, respiratory diseases, and nearly a dozen different types of cancer. Some studies even show that young people who smoke are more likely to compromise their health in a number of ways, such as fighting, carrying weapons, having unprotected sex, and abusing alcohol and other drugs.

Smoking has been linked to mental disorders just as other types of drug abuse have. One study found that adults who are depressed are 40% to 50% more likely to smoke than those who are not, and that adolescents who are depressed are more likely to continue smoking than those who aren't depressed. Depression also may make it harder to quit smoking. Other studies show a strong link between psychiatric illness and smoking in adolescents, but more research needs to be done in order to learn whether smoking increases risk for mental illness, or vice versa (or both).

I've gone into this detail about the various drugs of abuse not just to beat a drum about how and why they can wreak havoc on young people's lives. Chances are you've heard that drum before from others, and mine is only the latest in the band. But what you may not know is that treatment programs are often based on the type of drug or drugs abused, so it's important to understand the origins and nature of these substances and of an addiction to them when working on recovery. I'll talk about treatment in the next chapter, beginning with my story on how I finally got there.

Chapter Four

Trying to Get Help

There I was, on a wet New Jersey street, my parents' wrecked car upside down beside me. I had reached one of the lowest points in my life, and my situation was desperate. But in another respect, my dismal circumstances meant that if I were to keep on living, there was only one direction I could go, and that would have to be up. Eventually.

> *I had reached one of the lowest points in my life, and my situation was desperate.*

In this next chapter of my story, you'll see that I continued to have more downs than ups in my struggles to overcome my addiction, but my point in describing them at all is to show you something really important about treatment. Getting—and staying—clean doesn't happen in a day or a week or even a year. It's a constant, never-ending work in progress, and it has to begin with a serious commitment to get and stay clean.

That night I had no such commitment as yet. I was strapped to a gurney and taken to the hospital with a gash on my head and a couple of cracked and bruised ribs. They stitched up my head, but I walked out abruptly—even as they were still trying to work on me. My parents' car was on the back of a flatbed truck at some scrap mill. My shirt was covered in blood, I had a giant cut on my head, and I could barely breathe because my ribs were so sore. I called a friend to come get me. We put newspaper on the seat of his car so I wouldn't bleed all over it, then went back to the projects to buy heroin. I'd completely and utterly lost my mind.

I walked into the house that night to find my mother and father sitting at the dinner table with their heads in their hands. They looked at me and asked where the car was.

"You don't have a car anymore."

My parents had had it. They let me stay on their couch for two days, but I wasn't allowed to leave the house. Then I went back to detox.

Overconfidence and Denial: Do Not Mix

I went back to the facility I'd been to before for detox, then into a rehabilitation program where I stayed for 90 days, then to a halfway house in Westchester, New York. I was doing well. I had a sponsor and I was going to twelve-step meetings often enough that I had what is called a home group—a group where I was known and to which I unofficially belonged. I was working the steps, which I'll describe later but which, for now, simply meant that I was trying to improve my life. I got a full-time job and signed up for college, for a program in chemical dependency counseling. I got a girlfriend. I thought my life was in order. But I was overconfident, and made the mistake of thinking that staying sober would be easy. As anyone who has struggled to recover can tell you, underestimating the power of your addiction, plus personal overconfidence, can lead right to relapse.

And in fact that's what happened to me. I thought I had it made. I started slacking off and stopped going to meetings as much as I should. I started to resent the fact that I couldn't have a beer after work. My girlfriend was on the heavy and highly addictive painkiller OxyContin, which she took for pain from a broken leg. Also known as "hillbilly heroin" because of its chemical similarity to that drug, OxyContin is a very potent opioid. She was on a high dosage and before long I was taking it, too. I should have known that merely being around such a powerful narcotic was a mistake for someone like me, trying to overcome a heroin addiction. It was like an alcoholic thinking he could hang out in a bar without eventually giving in and having a drink.

And so, just like always, everything good in my life soon went away. I repeated the same old mistakes all over again. No more halfway house, no more college, no more job. All that went right out the window.

Around this time, I started having panic attacks. I began to struggle with anxiety and depression. I abused many different prescription medications, and mixed OxyContin with benzodiazapines—mild tranquilizers. I went on methadone to try and combat my new addiction to OxyContin.

I started having blackouts, and finally I had my first overdose. It's actually surprising that it didn't happen sooner. One morning I woke up and took a couple of OxyContins and some Xanax, a medication prescribed to combat anxiety. I blacked out, and still don't really know what happened after that. Apparently I had taken a number of different drugs, including heroin. When my girlfriend came home from work, she found me lying on her kitchen floor with a pot boiling over on the stove and empty pill bottles scattered everywhere, along with spoons caked with different substances that I'd tried to cook down. Needles were lying around, too. She yelled my name, thinking I was dead, and I jumped right up. My eyes were lifeless, she later told me, and she was scared just to look at me. Whoever was running my body was definitely not me. I ran out the door and into the apartment building's elevator, where I passed out.

The next thing I knew, I was waking up on a bed in the emergency room, a doctor peering down at me and saying I was lucky to be alive. "You're the first person we've ever had to administer six shots of Narcan to." Narcan is a drug that is used to counter the effects of an opioid overdose. Apparently most people come around with one or two shots; it had taken three times that to revive me.

I was angry at being awakened, because now I needed to get high again to avoid going into withdrawal. I felt like dying might have been preferable to waking up. I was belligerent with the doctor. "Who asked you to help me?" I yelled. I got up, ripped off all the tubes, and marched out of the hospital with my girlfriend behind me trying to convince me to go back. I made her give me the keys to her car, drove down to the Bronx, and bought ten bags of heroin. I remember reaching out the car window for the bags and seeing that I still had on the hospital bracelet, and I didn't care. That's the level of insanity I had reached. I didn't care that my need for drugs had, once again, spiraled completely out of control.

A Minor Arrest

Not long after that trip to the Bronx, I was coming back home from the same neighborhood by train when I happened to get off at the wrong stop. I was in a very altered state of mind, and disoriented. I realized my mistake and turned around to get back on the train, but it had already left without my noticing. Instead of boarding, I stepped right off the edge of the platform and fell down onto the tracks below. Amazingly, I didn't hurt myself, but it wouldn't be long before another train came through. People nearby pulled me back up onto the platform, but a police officer happened to see the whole thing. I'm sure the fall and my odd behavior made him suspicious, so he searched me.

I had a dirty needle on me and it was enough for the cop to arrest me. I'd been arrested before, of course—once when I stole that money from my mother's glove box, another few times for petty crimes like shoplifting. I'd always been released within a few days at most. But this time it was a month before I could get out. I was put on methadone in jail, and over the course of two weeks, my dosage was gradually lowered. Of all the withdrawals I've experienced, this was the most difficult. I'd never been so cold in my life. I don't know that I slept more than two hours on any given night during that time. I had no appetite and I was depressed to the point of wanting nothing but to die. It was a nightmare.

When I'd completed 30 days in jail, I thought that I would be released, but the court had discovered that I was in violation of my probation. That probation, for stealing my parents' money, had been for three years, but I hadn't reported to an officer as I was supposed to and had actually gone missing (while I was in California), so the probation clock had stopped. Instead of being released, I was transferred to the Orange County Jail, where I sat for another month awaiting the arraignment for violating probation.

By now I was off methadone and feeling a little better. I decided to let the judge know that I'd appreciate one more chance to try and get clean. Though I'd been before him twice, he agreed to release me to a therapeutic community—a treatment center where I'd live and receive counseling and support for an extended period of time.

A Major Arrest

I had never been exposed to this type of intensive drug treatment, and I went with the best of intentions. I decided that I'd try hard to devote myself to recovery. I was taught a type of therapy called *behavior modification,* in which responses to certain stimuli are altered through use of positive and negative reinforcement; the therapy was entirely new to me. I'd never been asked to scream at the top of my lungs, "Please help me." I'd never had to practice the sorts of mental and emotional exercises that drug addicts like me learned to help overcome their addictions.

I had to work to earn my keep, and I was subjected to strict disciplinary rules followed by all of the community's clients. I did well, and in time, I was given a job tutoring fellow clients who were working on their high school equivalency degrees, instructing them in algebra and science and English. I took pride in this job. At this same time, I also made one of my closest friends.

Again, I think I became overconfident and didn't admit how deep into the addiction I was. I was given a job as a driver, and the freedom of being able to leave the facility without supervision proved too much. I used my driving privileges to break the rules—I snuck out at night and bought alcohol, or bought it while on a drive with a group of residents. I never got caught for these infractions, and was eventually able to leave the treatment center and get a decent job. For a while I was considered a success story, but this was short-lived. Eventually I made the same old bad decisions. Soon I was completely back where I started, and it wasn't long before I was caught with 35 bags of heroin coming out of the same projects that I had lived in earlier—a major arrest.

I was charged with four felonies and a misdemeanor, and was sent to jail on $50,000 bond. I didn't even call home. My girlfriend had to call my parents to let them know. I spent three months straight in the very rough Passaic County Jail. I got into some altercations, but for the most part I held my own. I pled guilty to one count of third-degree criminal possession, a felony, but amazingly, I was given only three years probation. That meant that I didn't have to go back to jail, but I did have to meet with a probation officer regularly for drug tests and to ensure that I wasn't engaging in more criminal activity.

When I got out on probation, everyone figured I was "scared straight." But even that awful experience wasn't deterrent enough to keep me from my bad habits, and because I had taken no steps to change the rottenness growing inside of me, naturally I started to fall back into the same old patterns.

As part of my probation, I had to seek treatment on an outpatient basis. When I went to the initial outpatient interview, I confessed that I had relapsed and it was recommended that I go to a rehabilitation program. I was sent to a rehab center where I spent several months in inpatient treatment. The program allowed me to work my way through levels of privilege and freedom. First I was let out for 15 minutes a day, then, when I had mastered that amount of responsibility, I was allowed out for the weekend. Over the course of about a year and a half, I worked my way through the stages of the treatment program until I was finally released.

Up, Down, Up, Down—The Saga
of Addiction Continues

Around this time, I developed aspirations of becoming a commercial diver and started reading about the profession. It had intrigued me ever since my father had told me about the Navy SEALs all those years before. I was trying to map out a career and a future and I decided to go to school to qualify for underwater welding and commercial diving. But I wasn't doing anything to correct my real problem, the same old bad emotional feelings of emptiness and confusion that led me to abuse drugs. I was back to drinking secretively on weekends, even though I was just about to be released from probation. I was approved to go to school for commercial diving and everything looked good. But because I had no discipline or structure, because I had no ultimate desire or motivation to stay clean, and because I had taken no steps to correct the things that were wrong in my life and inside of me, I ended up using again. I got caught by my probation officer right before my probation was set to end and I was to leave for diving school.

By now, my addiction had gotten so bad that as soon as I started using again after a break, I would pick up right where I had left off and progress rapidly. I had been working, doing a little bit of carpentry and a little bit of landscaping when I could. But I wasn't very productive because most of my time I spent just driving back and forth to New Jersey or New York City to get heroin. Every time I went on a probation visit, I would think, "This is going to be it, this is the end." If I violated probation one more time and appeared in front of the judge in New Jersey again, I could be re-arraigned on all the original charges for my crimes in New Jersey. I could

I would think, "This is going to be it, this is the end."

have faced four felony charges, two second-degree, which meant a mandatory minimum of six years in prison. I was so far gone that I didn't care. I went to probation meetings high, practically asking to be caught, to be sent away, just to make this misery end.

I met my future wife around this time and tried to hold things together when we started dating, but it just didn't work, and we only dated for a short while. We felt that there was something strong between us, but she knew that nothing could happen as long as I was in such a desperate state.

Then, finally, I saw my probation officer one day and my drug test came back positive. I remember thinking, stupidly, "This is bad. How am I going to buy more heroin now?"

For some unknown reason, I wasn't arrested. Instead, I was told to drive myself to a crisis unit, the same place I'd been going to on and off for two years now. I was given half an hour to go to my apartment and pick up some belongings. But being so far gone, the first thing I did was hop in my car and go buy some drugs. I made it to the crisis unit at about two in the morning, completely obliterated, completely intoxicated. I knew this would probably be my last run for a long time.

A Crucial Turning Point

Because addiction is a chronic, relapsing disease that causes changes in the brain, getting well all by myself was essentially impossible. All those relapses you've just read about—all those painful, tedious, repetitive returns to the disastrous addiction—are part of the disease, and it had caused me and those who cared about me enormous misery. At the same time, every detox, every stint in a rehab facility, and even my many months in the treatment center had all been forced upon me. They'd been mandated by my parents, by courts, by probation officers. I was not at all happy about going into treatment the first time—or even the first several times. This too is part of the disease: Research shows that while treatment can help people stop abusing drugs or alcohol even if they don't enter it voluntarily, many people may need to undergo treatment more than once in order to stop using.

More to the point, though, is the need to commit not just to treatment but to recovery. I had never willingly chosen to fully commit myself to recovery, so I hadn't recovered. I believe a lot of people are mistaken in thinking that drug treatment is something that can be done *for* or perhaps even *to* an addict, when in fact it's really something an addict has to engage in willingly. Until I made the personal choice to embrace sobriety, instead of being ordered to, I'd never get free of my addiction. So, in a way, all of the time I'd previously spent in treatment, half-heartedly trying to quit using drugs, had been wasted, because I hadn't really wanted to quit.

This time, it was different. What I didn't know when I arrived at the crisis unit was that it would lead to a time of real change when I would be ready to put my last ounce of resolve into recovery, and that resolve is what ultimately made the difference between failure and success. I wish I could say why I made the decision to commit myself to getting clean this time. Maybe it was because I thought I'd finally hit rock bottom and had seen my own death staring me in the face. Maybe it was because I realized what I was doing to my loved ones by living so dangerously, or because I realized I couldn't be with my future wife unless I got clean. Or maybe it was simply because I was ultimately sent to a long-term treatment center and I didn't have any other choice but to stop using drugs and spend a lot of time thinking about all the mistakes I'd made. Whatever it was, it seemed to have worked. I was ready to accept that

I wouldn't be around much longer, given the direction I was headed.

Still, when I first went into recovery, after having been using drugs for so long, my mind was warped. I couldn't think rationally or logically. My outlook on life was completely negative. Everything I saw around me was negative. It seemed everyone was out to get me, and that nobody had my best interests at heart. I'd gravitate toward the negative and was just a miserable person. I was in the crisis facility for a week or two, then in detox, and then my treatment team chose a therapeutic community for me—a more difficult and demanding one than I was accustomed to, with a reputation for having the strictest discipline. It was in northern upstate New York, many miles from home.

At this point, I couldn't even imagine going into treatment again. I'd lost count of how many times I've been in treatment for the past nine years. Thirty detoxes? How many rehab stays? I'd run through three or four halfway houses and at least two or three outpatient treatment programs. What I didn't know was that I was starting a treatment program that would be the one to finally help me change.

What I didn't know was that I was starting a treatment program that would be the one to finally help me change.

Substance Abuse Treatment: What to Expect

Okay, let's zero in on what "treatment" means exactly. As you've seen from my story so far, there are different types of substance abuse treatment, but I haven't told you very much about what each type practically entails. Also, for young people who are under 18, or still in college, treatment tends to be a bit different from mine was as an adult in my twenties. Specialists have developed treatment programs that are designed specifically for young people whose living situations, levels of independence, and severity of drug use are most likely different from those of adults. The treatment center I was sent to in northern upstate New York was just about the most intensive type of substance abuse program there is, and most adolescents won't progress far enough into an addiction to necessitate such a program. So, while in the following sections I'll talk about various treatment settings and approaches by way of introducing you to much of what's available out there generically for people with a substance abuse problem, I'll emphasize aspects of them that are particularly relevant to young people like yourself.

First Step: Referral and Assessment

Most adolescents are referred to substance abuse treatment—that is, someone recognizes that a drug problem is present and recommends that the adolescent go into treatment. That someone could be a parent, a teacher, a counselor, or a doctor. If the teen has been in trouble with the law, oftentimes it's the juvenile justice system that mandates drug treatment (whereas in my case, it was the adult justice system that ordered that I go into treatment).

Once a referral to a treatment program has been deemed necessary, another decision must be made: what type of treatment program is best for this particular person and his or her substance abuse problem. There are many different treatment programs all over the country, and each one is unique, but most fall into one of the following categories:

- Detoxification
- Outpatient treatment

- Intensive outpatient treatment
- Residential treatment
- Aftercare

Treatment programs may be conducted within a hospital, at a community mental health center, or a specialized addiction treatment center. Because there are so many different kinds of facilities and programs, a careful and thorough assessment of your needs is an important step in making a good choice among treatment options. A professional well-versed in adolescent substance abuse should conduct this assessment to determine the appropriate level and type of treatment for you. (See the Resources section of this book for information on how to find professionals in your area who specialize in substance abuse.) The assessment should consider a number of things, including:

- Your age, gender, and maturity level
- The types of drugs you are abusing
- The intensity of use: Are you experimenting? Getting into problematic use? Addicted?
- How well or poorly you are functioning in various areas of your life
- The state of your relationships with family and friends: Have they deteriorated or are they still in good repair?
- Your level of responsibility: Do you need—for your safety or for that of others—a level of supervision and structure that your family cannot provide?
- Your emotional and psychological state: Do you need treatment for a co-occurring psychiatric condition?

The worse the drug abuse is—and addressing these concerns helps determine how far the abuse has progressed—the more support and supervision you'll need from a treatment program.

Detoxification

Actually, this is not a treatment in and of itself, but for many people who have become physically and psychologically addicted to any substance, treatment usually commences with detoxification, the process over several days of systematically withdrawing a person from addicting substances under medical supervision. Detox usually takes place in a special facility, and an individual's condition and circumstances will dictate whether he or she is an inpatient (living at the facility) or outpatient (visiting the facility on a regular schedule).

Those with a full-fledged addiction will experience withdrawal during the detoxification process, though it's likely that most adolescents' drug abuse hasn't progressed far enough for them to experience withdrawal. For heavy users of alcohol, barbiturates (a type of depressant), benzodiazepines, and for users of some other drugs, the effects of withdrawal can be dangerous and even lethal, so supervised detox may be a medical necessity. Sometimes legal medications are prescribed to addicts in detox to ease the withdrawal process, but again, this is usually seen only in older people. *Methadone* and *buprenorphine* are synthetic opioids prescribed for heroin addicts because they ease withdrawal symptoms and sometimes reduce cravings for heroin. *Methadone clinics* are usually outpatient facilities where addicts can obtain methadone on a regular basis without checking into the hospital. Detox is safest and most effective when overseen by doctors whose experience and training equips them to understand not only the physiological but also the psychiatric aspects of intoxication with the drug in question.

Getting the addictive substances out of a person's system is the first step in dealing with addiction, but again, detox is not to be considered a part of treatment. It doesn't

Getting the addictive substances out of a person's system is the first step in dealing with addiction...

do anything to help the person cope with all those brain cells that are still screaming for the drug. You'll remember that my family and I had this misconception the first time I went to detox. As my story shows, detox is virtually useless unless it is followed by some sort of drug treatment consisting of therapy or rehabilitation.

Outpatient Treatment

Treatment in which you continue to live at home but get a few hours of therapy during the day is known as *outpatient treatment*. Good adolescent outpatient treatment consists of a combination of individual counseling, group and family therapies, educational interventions such as lectures on addiction, and aftercare (follow-up treatment). Many include relapse prevention interventions, too. This many-pronged assault against substance abuse has been shown to be most successful in helping young people to get clean. Urine drug testing is usually a part of the deal, since the professionals in charge of the therapy will want to make sure you stay abstinent. Participation in groups like Alcoholics Anonymous (AA) or Narcotics Anonymous (NA) is encouraged. The activities involved in outpatient treatment will occur several times a week, but after recovery and abstinence have been maintained for a while, sessions and lectures may occur less often.

There are outpatient substance abuse programs of many different kinds nationwide. Some specialize in specific groups, like

Alcoholics Anonymous and Its Offspring

As part of your treatment program, you may be encouraged to attend support meetings like Alcoholics Anonymous (AA). Its famous twelve-step approach was first developed many years ago, and thousands of alcoholics have since recovered by actively taking each step in its course of redemption. The steps refer heavily to God, but AA is not associated with any specific religion, and members interpret its emphases on a higher power and spirituality according to their own beliefs:

1. *We admitted we were powerless over alcohol (our addiction)—that our lives had become unmanageable.*
2. *We came to believe that a Power greater than ourselves could restore us to sanity.*
3. *We made a decision to turn our will and our lives over to the care of God as we understood Him.*
4. *We made a searching and fearless moral inventory of ourselves.*
5. *We admitted to God, to ourselves, and to another human being the exact nature of our wrongs.*
6. *We were entirely ready to have God remove all these defects of character.*
7. *We humbly asked Him to remove our shortcomings.*
8. *We made a list of all persons we had harmed and became willing to make amends to them all.*
9. *We made direct amends to such people wherever possible, except when to do so would injure them or others.*
10. *We continued to take a personal inventory and when we were wrong promptly admitted it.*
11. *We sought through prayer and meditation to improve our conscious contact with God as we understood Him, praying only for knowledge of His will for us and the power to carry that out.*
12. *Having had a spiritual awakening as the result of these steps, we tried to carry this message to alcoholics (addicts) and to practice these principles in all our affairs.*

Though I never participated formally in AA, I did attend group therapy while in treatment that was philosophically based on the AA approach. In fact, AA has spawned similar groups like Narcotics

(continued)

Anonymous, for those recovering from drug addictions, and Al-Anon and Alateen, for those whose lives are affected by a loved one's alcohol abuse.

There are frequent AA and NA meetings in most communities across the United States; in larger cities, a meeting can probably be found almost every night and during the day on weekends. This is so that recovering addicts can have access to the supportive environment of the group whenever they feel they need it. Members of many different religions and of no religion attend meetings, and all are welcome. You can attend a meeting and elect not to share your story, instead listening to the discussions of others. Meetings can usually be found through your local Yellow Pages, or online. See the Resources section of this book for information on how to find an AA or NA meeting near you.

adolescents, women, or people with HIV/AIDS. Many offer multiple language services for those who don't speak English, and some offer detox services. Most accept a wide range of payment methods, including cash, insurance, and Medicaid; some use a sliding fee scale for those with limited financial resources.

Let's take a closer look at each of the components of a good adolescent outpatient treatment program.

Individual Counseling

Individual counseling, or *psychotherapy* (also called "talk therapy"), targets the psychological, social, and behavioral aspects of a given mental illness or problem, including substance abuse. For the majority of young people, taking the time to discuss a substance abuse problem with a counselor or therapist can be enormously helpful in discovering why the abuse is happening and how it can be healthfully stopped. This type of therapy can be conducted by a psychologist, a psychiatrist, a social worker, or a specially trained substance abuse counselor, and is especially appropriate when teens are living with their parents. Counseling usually takes place in several sessions per week and may employ different methods of therapy. Following are some of the major methods.

- **Behavioral therapies** are based upon the idea that substance abusers are more able to change their destructive use of drugs if they are able to recognize and realize the benefits of *not* using drugs. Adolescents in behavioral therapy might complete writing assignments on their drug use, engage in role-playing with therapists to better understand the consequences of drug abuse, and sometimes even receive small awards when sobriety is maintained.
- **Cognitive-behavioral therapy**, or CBT, is a type of psychotherapy that aims to correct ingrained patterns of thinking and behavior that may be contributing to a given disorder, such as substance abuse. Unrealistic, negative ideas and pessimistic attitudes are identified and reframed in more realistic or optimistic terms. *Maladaptive* (harmful and destructive) behaviors are modified to make enjoyment of everyday activities more possible. For a teenager with a substance abuse problem, CBT might examine the unhappy thought patterns that precede drug use. CBT is one of the most effective therapeutic approaches in adults with substance abuse, and a study conducted in 2001 showed that CBT was effective for adolescents, too.

> CBT is one of the most effective therapeutic approaches in adults with substance abuse...

- **Interpersonal therapy**, or IPT, is a method that has proven effective in adults, but researchers are hopeful that it also helps adolescents. It is based on the idea that, even though a wide number of factors may lead to a given disorder (like addiction), it is often an interpersonal or social problem that triggered it. Changes in social roles and poor social skills might increase risk for substance abuse, especially in young teens for whom dependence on a social network and the importance of being *cool* are so vital. IPT for young people who are abusing drugs might focus on developing social skills so that a teen need not rely on drug use to make friends.

I should mention that I'm throwing around terms like *counseling* and *psychotherapy* pretty interchangeably, as though they mean the same thing. From your point of view, they do, in the sense that they're focusing on helping you to understand and overcome your problems. But there are some differences between them. Generally speaking, counseling tends to focus on learning about a specific problem and how to deal with it. Substance abuse counseling, for example, emphasizes learning about drugs and addiction, evaluating your own patterns of use, and figuring out ways to address them. Psychotherapy, on the other hand, emphasizes helping you understand your feelings and actions on a deeper level so that you can make positive changes in your approach to life. Clearly, though, counseling and therapy are not two completely separate activities but rather two parts of a greater whole. Nor are they confined to individual outpatient treatment, but are also used with groups, including with families, and in residential treatment settings.

The types of counseling and therapy used in a program depend on the philosophy of the facility, the training of its staff, and the treatment approaches that appear best for the individual.

Within the various treatment settings, professionals will use a number of therapeutic methods and approaches to help you understand how addictive substances have affected your brain, body, and behavior; how stopping their use affects you; and how you can learn to overcome those effects and live your life without them. They can also help you to look into your feelings and motivations to find out why you might have felt you needed drugs, and how you can meet those needs in healthy ways. You can relearn—or learn for the first time—how to deal with life challenges and the people around you. You can also learn to deal with the stresses that can trigger relapse.

Alphabet Soup: Ph.D.? M.D.? M.S.W.?

Several different types of professionals provide care for those with a substance abuse problem; each group has its own educational and licensing requirements, and each practitioner has a unique set of skills he or she can use to help you in your treatment.

- *Psychiatrists* (M.D.s) are medical doctors who are trained to diagnose and treat mental disorders and emotional problems. Psychiatrists may specialize in one or more areas of mental health, such as child and adolescent psychiatry, or addiction psychiatry, and can prescribe medication if necessary.
- *Clinical psychologists* (Ph.D.s) provide assessment and psychotherapy for mental and emotional disorders.
- *Clinical social workers* (M.S.W.s) provide psychotherapy as well but also tend to focus on improving conditions in one's environment that might be contributing to that person's problems.
- *Addiction specialists* may have one or more advanced degrees and have undergone specialized training in order to become a certified substance abuse counselor.

Group Therapy

In group therapy, participants gather to discuss a particular shared problem, such as substance abuse, in an environment of support and mutual understanding. Usually guided by a trained professional, group therapy allows young people to see that they are not alone in their struggles with substance abuse, and to learn techniques from each other on maintaining sobriety. For teens, this peer-group approach can be especially effective, and has been scientifically shown to help adolescents reduce their substance abuse. Like individual therapy, group therapy is usually conducted as part of a larger treatment plan, and may take place either on an outpatient basis or within the confines of a more intensive treatment program. Note that this type of professionally led group arrangement is not the same as mutual-help groups like AA or NA, which tend to be run by their own members.

Family Therapy

Because teens, especially younger ones, are usually living at home with their parents when they first start experimenting with drugs, engaging the entire family in therapy is often seen as an integral part of the recovery process. The family, including the teen, the parents, and maybe even siblings, meet both as a group and individually with the therapist as a way of examining the teen's substance abuse problem "in the round"—that is, in the context of the family unit. The therapy often focuses on communication skills, changing destructive patterns that may be contributing to the substance abuse, strengthening family bonds, and reducing conflict at home. The family-based approach is among the most widely studied by researchers and has been shown to be highly effective in getting teens to reduce their abuse of substances.

Educational Interventions

Outpatient treatment often incorporates lessons and lectures on drugs, addiction, the brain, and so on, so that young people in recovery can educate themselves on the dangers of drug use. These are also known as *psychoeducational interventions.* Sometimes adolescents are given writing or research assignments to broaden their knowledge of substance abuse issues; I myself wrote a paper on the science of addiction while I was in treatment. Incorporating psychoeducational interventions into adolescent substance abuse treatment has been shown to increase success rates.

Relapse Prevention Interventions

Many outpatient treatment programs also focus on preventing relapse, which becomes very important once you leave the highly supportive environment of the treatment program. Oftentimes, young people are taught how to respond sensibly to the *people, places, and things* previously associated with their substance abuse. For example, you might learn both how to identify high-risk situations that could increase the likelihood that you'll use drugs and how to cope with such situations. You might also be taught *lifestyle modification strategies* that give you alternatives to drug use, like meditation, exercise, and developing spiritual interests. I'll talk more about relapse and recovery in Chapter 5.

Intensive Outpatient Treatment

Intensive outpatient treatment incorporates all of the same elements as outpatient treatment, but usually lasts a full day, and frequently includes the addition of school-like sessions during the day. Since so many hours are taken up by intensive outpatient treatment, adolescents are often absent from regular school for an extended period of time. In order to ensure that they don't fall behind their classmates academically, lessons in subjects like math, science, writing, and English are taught alongside the substance abuse treatment sessions.

Residential Treatment

The treatment that finally allowed me to get my life back involved spending a year in a residential facility designed to deal with my problems and to help me learn to cope. In a residential treatment setting, the addict lives for an extended period of time in a house-like setting with other addicts, overseen by professionals trained to facilitate the recovery process. A stay in residential treatment can be short-term, lasting only a few weeks, or long-term, lasting at least a year. At its most intense, residential treatment involves a highly structured schedule in which residents participate in a number of activities, such as substance abuse counseling and education, going to school, doing chores, and taking part in recreation. As the treatment progresses, more and more privileges are allowed until the addict leaves the residence.

Because it is so costly, residential treatment is usually only accessible to those families with ample financial resources, to people with multiple failed attempts at outpatient treatment, or to those who have been mandated to treatment (often as an alternative to prison) by the justice system. In this last case, the addict may be jailed if he or she leaves the residence without permission, or fails to follow rules and complete treatment activities. In other words, residential treatment is often considered a treatment of last-resort for people who have exhausted all other options. Few adolescents will ever need to turn to residential treatment for this reason.

Aftercare

Follow-up treatment after the recovery program, be it outpatient or residential, is typically referred to as *aftercare,* and is usually comprised of attendance at an aftercare group once a week or every two weeks, combined with urine tests and occasional individual counseling. Research in adolescent substance abuse has shown that active participation in aftercare is the best predictor of a successful recovery.

In my opinion, aftercare is crucial to maintaining recovery.

I can't stress enough the importance of aftercare. Time and again, I refused the option of aftercare when I left treatment, and the result was always the same: relapse. In my opinion, *aftercare is crucial to maintaining recovery.*

Determining the Right Treatment Setting for You, and Finding It

Sorting through the different types of treatment programs and facilities can get pretty confusing, and finding which one is the right one for you can take time. I had been to a whole lot of them, but until the last one, none had really met my needs. It was my good luck, finally, that the probation staff chose a facility that was a match for my addiction, and that their choice coincided with my decision—finally—to commit to getting clean. For treatment to work, it has to fit your level of substance abuse, but it also has to fit the kind of person you are, meet your particular needs, and address the issues that matter to you. For example, for a teenager, a treatment setting must:

- Be appropriate to your age. Teens and adults differ in many ways, and programs designed for adults are often not right for teens. Teenagers are at a different developmental stage than adults; their brains are still maturing and their thinking follows somewhat different patterns.
- Be appropriate for your life circumstances and living situation. Teenagers generally live at home with their parents and are dependent on them. Treatment programs designed for teens, especially younger ones, tend to involve the parents and perhaps other family members as well. In most cases they do not involve living away from home, but rather attending a series of therapy sessions after school or in the evenings. There are exceptions to this, however, as when the drug abuse is endangering the teen and others, and a more supportive environment like residential treatment is needed to keep everyone safe.
- Match the treatment to the severity of substance abuse. Teenagers, especially younger ones, are often less deeply involved in addictive substances and may be less likely than older people to have moved all the way to severe, long-term addiction. This may simply reflect the shorter amount of time that they have had to use drugs and the fact that they probably have less opportunity and less money than older people, and probably more scrutiny and supervision by their parents, teachers, and others. Regardless, it's important that the treatment program recognize that your problems are unique, and help you to solve them in ways that work for you.
- Offer treatment for any and all psychiatric disorders you may have (more on this shortly).

What all of this means is that not every program designed for teens is right for every teenager. The teen years cover a tremendous developmental span. Treatment that suits you at 13 might be inappropriate for you at 18, and vice versa. Younger teens tend to be pretty concrete in their thinking and less considerate of long-term consequences than older teens, who think much more abstractly, and treatment providers need to take this into account. Many other features of our lives—such as relations with our peer groups and with the opposite sex, plus our levels of independence—also change a lot between the ages of 13 and 18.

Gender is another factor that can make a big difference in whether treatment is effective, since guys and girls have some very different experiences and concerns and face some very different issues. Research shows, for example, that adolescent girls who abuse substances are much more likely than boys to have experienced sexual or physical abuse and to suffer severe family problems. Clearly, their treatment must address the issues that come out of those experiences if they've had them. That doesn't mean that coed programs can't be successful, but it does mean that they have to give people of both genders the chance to work on the issues that matter to them.

Treatment programs involve various kinds of psychological therapies and, if appropriate, medications as well. Depending on the substance issues, medications may also play an important role for a limited number of young people. Buprenorphine, for example, was crucial in allowing me to finally get off heroin.

Actually finding the treatment center that is right for you can take a little legwork. Social service agencies, schools, your primary care doctor, and even your local hospital can be good

Medications Used in Addiction Treatment

Over the years, the notion of treating addiction with prescription medication has gained popularity and scientific support. Unfortunately, at this time most drugs prescribed to treat addiction have only been tested in adults, so doctors must carefully consider whether prescribing these medications to adolescents is warranted. Also, prescription drug treatment, or *pharmacotherapy,* has some limitations. Prescription drugs may help reduce the cravings and withdrawal symptoms that so often derail recovery, but they won't help you with comorbid psychiatric issues like depression or PTSD. Also, medications are available only for addiction to heroin and alcohol, but not as yet for treatment of addiction to other substances like marijuana or ecstasy.

For opioid addiction

- *Methadone*—long-acting opioid *agonists* (replacements for the drug of abuse) that fill receptors affected by heroin, but do not cause a "high."
- *Buprenorphine*—a potent opioid agonist with a chemical structure similar to morphine that blocks heroin at the receptor
- *Naltrexone*—helps prevent heroin relapse, known as an opioid *antagonist* (it inhibits the action of the drug of abuse).

For alcohol addiction

- *Acamprosate*—reduces craving for alcohol.
- *Naltrexone*—helps prevent alcohol cravings and reduces the risk of an alcohol binge.
- *Disulfiram (Antabuse)*—destroys one of the body's natural chemicals, an enzyme that breaks down alcohol. Drinking alcohol after taking this drug produces an unpleasant physical reaction characterized by headache, nausea, vomiting, dizziness, and trouble breathing. Disulfiram is rarely prescribed to adolescents because they are more likely to consume alcohol despite the unpleasant aftereffects, which can be harmful to their health.

Actually finding the treatment center that is right for you can take a little legwork.

sources of information about the treatment options available in your area. The Internet is also a good way to search for information. For example, the Substance Abuse and Mental Health Services Administration (SAMHSA) sponsors a search engine you can use to find treatment providers near you. See the Resources section of this book for more information.

Treatment of Co-occurring Mental Disorders

Psychiatric disorders like those I discussed in Chapter 2 can seriously complicate the treatment of a substance abuse problem. In many cases, the underlying mental disorder helps to nourish the substance abuse, so any serious attempt to treat the substance abuse must also address any and all psychiatric issues if true recovery is to be achieved. If you started using drugs to relieve some feeling of sadness and emptiness within you, then you probably won't be able to stay away from drugs in the future unless you take the time now to tackle those bad feelings, find out where they are coming from, and work to make them go away. You can see an example of this in my own story; over and over again I tried my hand at recovery without admitting to myself that I was using drugs to escape from my own bad feelings of failure, self-loathing, and emotional discomfort. Only when I did bite the bullet and face these problems did my recovery stick. In other words, you could have access to the best substance abuse treatment in the world, but if you don't work on your mental health issues too, it won't do you any good.

Unfortunately, as if getting help for substance abuse alone wasn't hard enough, teenagers who also have a psychiatric problem (known as a *dual diagnosis* in mental health circles) can face some real challenges when seeking out treatment. Facilities offering substance abuse treatment often don't offer mental health services; on the other hand, many mental health providers don't offer substance abuse counseling. There are several reasons historically for this divide—among them the mistaken belief a long time ago that addicts *couldn't* benefit from psychological treatment—and its effects have lingered to this day, with two very different professions often operating independently of each other in the problems they recognize and in the people they're willing to treat. Those with the misfortune of having both sets of problems can end up a little like a half-tuned car.

A number of efforts have developed over the past several years to change this troubling trend; more and more, experts are recognizing that mental illness is a risk factor for substance abuse, and that they often go hand-in-hand. Research has shown that the prognosis for recovery is much brighter when substance abuse and psychiatric problems are treated simultaneously. Ultimately, it's best when a single institution knows how to deal with both issues, or when a pair of institutions has a well-established system of cooperating to combine their services. That said, getting the right combination of services is still not easy in many areas of the country. Some substance abuse treatment facilities flat-out refuse to accept people with mental health diagnoses, for instance. If you can, talk to your parents, a professional, or another trusted adult about any concerns you may have about your mental health, and how it might have affected your substance abuse. This may help shed some light on your situation, and help lead you to the proper treatment setting. For more information on how to find a treatment provider who can help you with these issues, see the Resources section of this book.

As you can see from all this, choosing the right treatment facility will take some work. I got into the program that finally helped me almost by dumb luck, if you want to call it that.

Paying for Treatment

Good treatment is not cheap. Substance abuse treatment facilities can be either private or public. Private facilities are more expensive because they usually do not rely on funding from the government. Public facilities are funded by the government and so are less expensive, sometimes even free—but often have long waiting lists for this very reason. The longer your stay in a treatment program, the more expensive it is likely to be.

My long residential stay was possible because the State of New York paid for it. Without public funding for my treatment, I very much doubt that I could have obtained it. My family is not wealthy, and there's no way that my parents could have paid for the months of treatment in a residential facility that I needed. I was too old to be included on their health insurance, and in any case it would be unusual for private health insurance to pay for such an extended period of treatment as mine.

Still, if you are under 18 or enrolled in a full-time college program, you may be eligible for coverage under your parents' plan. Substance abuse benefits available under health insurance plans do vary widely, so it's important that you or your parents take a careful look at whatever health insurance coverage they have to make sure that you get all the benefits you're entitled to. It's also important to demand that the insurance company pay for the detailed assessment necessary to choose a treatment facility. Under many insurance plans, those benefits are quite limited, as are benefits for mental health in general. You can always appeal any insurance company's decision to deny your claim for coverage, and it's said that about three out of every five appeals is granted.

In my home state of New York, many addicts are able to get substance abuse treatment under Medicaid; in other states, the benefits available under Medicaid vary. You should check your state's eligibility rules and benefits to see whether you qualify and what is available (see the Resources section of this book).

(continued)

If neither insurance nor Medicaid is an option for you, some treatment facilities will agree to charge you using a sliding scale; this means that their fee is based on your particular income and/or ability to pay. Others have payment assistance programs if you have limited financial resources. Be sure to research with your parents the different payment options available to you, and investigate whether there are free substance abuse treatment programs available in your community. A doctor, hospital, town department of health, or school counselor may be able to refer you to such programs.

Because I'd been arrested, I was under the jurisdiction of the criminal justice system, which in turn chose the facilities that I went to. Most of the time, the justice system will only be involved in treatment choices if there has been some sort of run-in with the law. And for most kids, it is their parents or other adults in their lives who arrange for treatment, and who first notice that it may be needed. Most communities have some kind of treatment program or programs for teens, and often mental health professionals such as clinical social workers, psychologists, psychiatrists, or family doctors make referrals to these programs.

I can't tell you exactly how your treatment will unfold because it depends on your own particular circumstances and on what type of treatment setting you choose. But I can tell you this. I know from my own experience that effective treatment can get you free of drugs and start teaching you the skills you'll need for the ride that comes next: living your life—hopefully, the rest of your life—in recovery.

Chapter Five

Recovery

P rior to going to the therapeutic community upstate, I went to detox and was given Suboxone (buprenorphine), which feels as though it burns the heroin right out of your system. No tolerance develops for it, nor is there any high. It prevented me from going into withdrawal and kept me from getting sick. And so, by the time I went upstate, I felt normal physically. But emotionally? That's another matter altogether. I was still a miserable, angry person—just in different surroundings.

As time went by, though, I started to look back at everything that I had been through, and that's really when I began to change. The therapeutic community ultimately allowed me to get my life back, to get into real recovery. It provided me with a place to be away from the street, away from the active addiction and the temptation of drugs always within such easy reach. Secluded as it was, it let me gather my thoughts; it let my mind begin to heal.

Over the course of a year, I dealt with what they call *post-acute withdrawal syndrome,* a set of impairments that affect an addict's emotion regulation, memory, and cognitive (thinking and perception) abilities. During this time I went through a lot of different emotional and mental phases. Everything felt new. I was completely numb when I was using, so now I was dealing with unfamiliar emotions of intimacy and anger, and I wasn't adept at regulating either of them. I faced the question of how to deal with my anger constructively— and without drugs. Plus, this was a coed facility, so I was also dealing with feelings of sexual urgency that had come back in a strong way.

> I faced the question of how to deal with my anger constructively—and without drugs.

   As for the program itself, the therapists there used behavior modification techniques—a system of rewards and punishments for actions—that helped teach me self-discipline. As part of my therapy, I was given a little job to do, working in the legal department providing computer support. I also found other ways to keep busy and be constructive. This particular facility did not endorse the twelve-step meeting approach, but I knew it from previous times in treatment, so I got permission to conduct my own support group with fellow residents. We met two nights a week in the fashion of Narcotics Anonymous, although we weren't an official NA group. Still, the twelve-step programs define their meetings as two or more addicts coming together to help one another, and that's exactly what we did. In these meetings, we discussed many things of a personal nature—frustrations, concerns, problems, sometimes memories kept secret for a long time—and members would routinely break down into tears. The meetings turned out to be extremely valuable, therapeutically. The group started with about 15 people, but eventually grew to 25 or 30. We ultimately split into two groups in order to keep them small, personal, and intimate.

The facility's location made relapse difficult. In other treatment centers, all I had to do was walk out the door and go three blocks and I'd have what I wanted. But here, I was in the middle of nowhere. I was pretty much stuck. That certainly didn't erase the feelings and urges that could lead to using, though, so I know it's possible that I would have gotten high again if some heroin had been available. But I was learning to deal with these feelings constructively; I was learning that there were ways to deal with difficult emotions without turning to substance abuse. It was hard for me to believe, at first, that anything *besides* heroin could help ease the suffering I felt inside. But slowly I was developing the coping mechanisms that I'd use on the outside—ways of thinking that would help me not turn to drugs.

Eventually, after a year of substance abuse counseling, therapy, and intense soul-searching, it was time for me to leave the treatment facility and strike out on my own. This was a terrifying prospect at the time—still is, occasionally. But I couldn't stay there forever, and it was time for me to reclaim my life and see what the future had in store for me.

What Does Recovery Mean for You?

As you can see, recovery is much more than a physical or medical process. That aspect of it is important, of course, but an equally important element of recovery is its psychological dimension. It also involves discipline and specific techniques. In treatment, I learned a number of lessons on how to avoid returning to my old substance-abusing ways—to avoid relapse. Your experiences in recovery may not be quite like mine, since I was an adult by the time I was sent to the therapeutic community. Recovery from an adolescent perspective can look a bit different; the day-to-day life of a teen centers mostly around school, peers, activities, and families, so it's important to focus on these elements and understand how they play into your own efforts to stay off drugs.

So—you've left your treatment program. What comes next? Once your formal treatment is finished, a whole new set of challenges await you. Just because you're not attending substance abuse counseling every day anymore doesn't mean you can stop being vigilant about maintaining recovery and staying clean. You'll need to remember and use the strategies you learned to avoid relapse.

Dealing With Cravings and Urges to Use Drugs

It's one thing to avoid using drugs when there are none available, or when there's no one or nothing around to remind you of your drug-using days—out of sight, out of mind, right? It's another thing entirely to manage your cravings for substances when they're staring you in the face or when you're surrounded by friends you used to get high with. Here are some of the tricks—what previously I called *lifestyle modification strategies*—that I've used to reduce cravings and urges. A lot of these concepts are useful to people of all ages who've used drugs.

MAKE PLANS AND FIND ACTIVITIES THAT DON'T
INVOLVE DRUGS

The first time I realized that I might have some sort of dependence was years ago when, one night, my friends and I couldn't get our hands on any LSD. We thought our night was completely ruined. We said to each other over and over again, "We wouldn't use if there was something else to do around here. We only use because there's nothing else to do." But really, that wasn't the case. There was always something else we could

In recovery, it's important to stay busy, to make plans for small, fun things to do with family and friends who don't use drugs ...

have done with ourselves; we just didn't bother to think about what else we might do to pass the time. In recovery, it's important to stay busy, to make plans for small, fun things to do with family and friends who don't use drugs, and to develop new interests and activities so that drug use doesn't start to seem like the only way to enjoy yourself. Here are a few activities that I've found especially helpful:

- *Writing* in a journal and expressing myself through my writing have been very important to me throughout my recovery. Doing so yourself will occupy your mind and offer an outlet for emotional and psychological frustrations that might otherwise be kept bottled up inside of you—an unhealthy recipe for relapse. You never have to show your writing to anyone, but you may find that just getting your feelings out on paper has enormous therapeutic value.
- *Meditation* can help you manage emotions that sometimes become overwhelming. Anxiety, anger, depression—they can be hard to cope with, especially while in recovery, and the craving for drugs can get intense as emotions really start to erupt. I've learned to quiet my mind and meditate when life starts to feel too hectic or too chaotic to manage. Not religiously, not every day—but if I'm having a difficult time and starting to get anxious and angry, then I'll practice some calming breathing exercises and try to put myself into a state of relaxation. You can check out groups in

your community that teach meditative techniques; try your hand at yoga, for instance, which is a wholesome blend of low-impact physical activity and meditation.

- *Aerobic exercise* is also a great way to relieve tension and keep busy—plus it's one of the healthiest things you can do for yourself. There were times in rehab when I felt physically horrible. I'd been off drugs for weeks, but I still felt miserable. I took on an exercise routine and realized that working out would help my body and my mind recuperate quicker. Physical activity helped my brain re-learn to release endorphins without the help of harmful chemicals. Now I jog about two miles a couple of times a week and it feels great. It's almost like a natural high.

If you still find yourself unoccupied, with the boredom or drug cravings starting to creep in, visit a non-using friend or talk to someone you trust in your family. Better yet, plan lots of get-togethers throughout the week so that the boredom and cravings never have a chance to take hold. If you don't have one already, think about getting a part-time job to occupy your time; this has the added benefit of earning you some money, as well as pride in being a productive member of society. If you can't commit to regular employment, seek out volunteer opportunities in your community.

Steer Clear of the Bearers of Temptation
I work hard to avoid people, events, or situations that are associated with drugs or using and that trigger cravings. One of those situations, for example, is social drinking, and I no longer socialize with friends at bars. Even when I eventually went to diving school, I wouldn't join my fellow divers for a

drink after a day's training but instead would do something else, such as exercising or writing. Ironically, I got a reputation as a "straight edge" sort of guy who didn't touch the stuff!

One of the best ways to stay clean is to avoid environmental cues that can stimulate drug cravings. Don't visit places where you once used, and avoid socializing with people who still use drugs. If you have a ticket to a rock concert where you know everyone will be getting high, for example, you may have to consider not going if you truly want to maintain your recovery. Just the smell of marijuana can bring on intense cravings that you may not be able to resist—but you can resist going to the concert altogether. This can be one of the most difficult aspects of staying clean—giving up activities you once enjoyed. It's a hard choice to have to make, I know, but the costs of relapsing are high.

Many professionals suggest that you terminate friendships entirely with people who are still using. This may seem harsh, but it's in your best interest to separate yourself from people who may interfere with your recovery. The same goes for siblings—if your older brother, for example, routinely drinks or gets high, maybe it's best for you to avoid hanging out with him socially. Your reasons for staying away from him might even inspire him to get clean, too.

> ...it's in your best interest to separate yourself from people who may interfere with your recovery.

You might also seek out pro-abstinence social groups that by their nature won't pressure you to drink or get high. For most of us, especially when we're young, the opinion of others means a lot, so it would help your recovery to hang out with others who don't think it's especially cool to do drugs.

Seek Out Continuing Support and Treatment

One of the surest ways to maintain recovery is to continue with the therapy that helped you to get clean in the first place, and so it is vital to work out a plan for ongoing support after you leave treatment. A formal aftercare program usually requires regular attendance and is conducted by counselors or therapists. It can involve "booster" sessions, where you visit a treatment center to get an extra dose of the treatment experience to strengthen your recovery. It can also mean regular appointments with a psychotherapist to discuss daily life and to get help in managing stress and avoiding relapse. Especially when facing trouble, adversity, and setbacks, which everyone does from time to time, and when facing cravings, which all recovering substance abusers do, in recovery you need the support of those who can give you the strength to remain abstinent. I continue to see a psychotherapist myself to help sustain my recovery.

In fact, continuing therapy is especially important if you suffer from a comorbid psychiatric disorder, like depression or bipolar disorder. As we saw in Chapters 2 and 4, mental health issues that occur along with a substance abuse problem are often thought to contribute to the drug abuse, so treating these disorders is a must. If after you leave a treatment program, you can't continue to see a psychotherapist, seek out a local addiction support group and make a commitment to attend meetings regularly.

These of course could include Alcoholics Anonymous and Narcotics Anonymous, which I've already mentioned, but in some communities there are meetings especially for teenagers and young people. Whatever group, though, they're free and people can attend as often as they want or need in order gain support in their recovery process. In many cases, a person new to recovery will rely on a more experienced member, called a sponsor, for help with the twelve-step philosophy and the general issues of recovery.

Trying AA on for Size

Koren Zailckas describes an adolescence and young adulthood marked by alcohol abuse in her book, *Smashed.* By the closing pages, she's just graduated college, and come to accept that her troubled relationship with alcohol has robbed her of many of the most important memories and experiences of growing up. She attempts to seek help anonymously. Though this particular episode ends without Zailckas taking advantage of the help she's solicited, it does illustrate the sometimes circuitous route by which many people with a substance abuse problem try to deal with it.

I decide to take the doctor's advice and try an AA meeting. I call Alcoholics Anonymous, where I am referred to New York Intergroup, where a pleasant young operator reads me meeting times like movie times. I request AA groups in the East Village, which is more than seventy blocks from my apartment, so I won't have to worry about encountering alcoholics in the neighborhood post office or the produce aisle of the grocery store. Downtown, I also expect to find a younger crowd than the group of crusty old men that smoke Marlboro Reds in front of a meeting on East Eightieth Street.

Still, a curious thing happens when I show up at a church on Lafayette Street after work. The night is mild and the sidewalks are empty, save for the mass of people dallying under a sallow streetlight. They are all young, blue-jeaned, pink-cheeked, and tousle-haired. As I approach them, I can see they are calling out to one another and embracing. Some are dancing. More are blowing over the mouth-holes of their deli coffee cups. The scene is so kindly I panic. I don't know what I will say to this confederacy of cat-eyed extroverts wearing Army jackets and plastic earrings. When I reach the church entrance, I keep walking to the corner bookstore. I go inside and pretend to scan the racks for a rare volume of poetry. (Reprinted from Koren Zailckas, *Smashed: Story of a Drunken Girlhood* [New York: Viking, 2005].)

Finally, during your recovery, you may be able to benefit from prescription medications for certain conditions. As I mentioned in the last chapter, there is not a lot of research available at this time that proves that available addiction medications work for adolescents. Professionals are forced to rely on data in adult populations, and so most doctors will not prescribe them for young people except under very close scrutiny. On the other hand, medications for a psychiatric illness like depression, bi-polar disorder, or an anxiety disorder are readily prescribed now to adolescents, although necessarily still with close monitoring by a psychiatrist or other prescribing physician, so you may want to explore this option with your treatment provider. These meds, together with psychological support from a therapist and/or a support group, can help sustain your recovery.

Reentering Society

After having abused drugs for so long and once in recovery, you'll likely find it a challenge to fit in at home and school. Things may not be quite as you remembered them from your drug-using days, and it may take time to re-establish your role among those you know and love.

REBUILDING TRUST

As you've seen from my story, I hurt a lot of people while I was addicted to heroin; I lied, I stole from my parents, I broke the law over and over again. For a long time, my parents didn't trust me—and I can't blame them—nor did my non-using friends, or other people in my community who knew me and knew about the trouble I'd gotten into. In recovery I was forced to recognize that it would take some work for me to heal the hurt I'd caused and earn back the trust I'd thrown away.

You'll likely face this challenge as well, and you might despair that your loved ones will ever trust you again. But with a lot of hard work on your part to show you're committed meaningfully to a sustained recovery, you'll regain their trust in time. You may run into similar problems at school, where non-using peers may label you as a druggie or a loser. The chilling effect of this stigma can be quite painful, and, sadly, can make it even harder for you to stay clean. You may feel quite isolated for a while—you've rejected your drug-using friends in an attempt quit drugs, but those who never used them at all want nothing to do with you. Again, hard work and time can help you to overcome their prejudice. In the meantime, keep in touch with your therapist or support group to help you deal with these problems and avoid relapse during this rocky reentry period in your life.

BUILDING SELF-ESTEEM AND ACCEPTANCE

I have learned that a crucial step in recovery is learning to love and accept oneself.

I have learned that a crucial step in recovery is learning to love and accept oneself. Earlier I discussed how I felt inferior to other people, how nervous I was, an outsider who got picked on and wasn't popular. I didn't much like myself. I thought using drugs made me a better person, but then what I did to be that person was horrendous. As I stole from everyone I knew in order to get drugs, and as I plunged from bad to worse into my addiction and into the sordid life it spawned, the self-hatred built up more and more. When I finally stopped using for good, I was the last person I wanted to see looking back at me in the mirror. And so, one of the hardest steps in my own recovery was coming to terms with all the awful things that I'd done. But in doing so, and in trying to forgive myself, I had also to come to terms with *me.*

I remember thinking "I've got to get back to normal," and then, "Wait a minute, when have I ever been normal?" I wondered what I was working toward. Who was I trying to become? It was hard to envision achieving sobriety because I was basically trying to become someone that I had never been—a responsible adult who lives without drugs. One of the tragic things about addiction is that when you start using, your emotional growth as a person screeches to a halt, even regresses. I started abusing drugs when I was 16, so I still had the emotional maturity of a teenager when I stopped using as a young man. I had a lot of growing up to do. That meant figuring out who I was in the first place and then accepting myself.

In adolescence, finding one's separate identity is all part of growing up. My wish for you is that you'll find yours faster than I did mine, and that in recovery you'll embrace your right to be you. You've lost some time to whatever substance caught you, but having screwed up the courage to break its grip, you can now move on to look into a mirror and really know what it means to like what you see.

Keeping Recovery on the Agenda

Not a day goes by that I don't think about recovery. It is a way of life for me now. That said, I can never forget that I'm an addict. I have to maintain constant vigilance against the threat of relapse, as does any recovering addict. Not too long ago a phone conversation with an old friend took a turn toward reminiscing about the past. "Remember when . . . ?" I saw the conversation going in a direction that I did not want or need to go. Drug use can bring about an effect known as *euphoric recall.* That's when a drug addict remembers only how good using the drug felt, and not how badly he or she acted while high, nor the negative consequences of being high. Make no mistake—your memories of drug use, under the right conditions, *can* trigger a relapse. Recognizing this hard fact is one of the key steps in preventing relapse.

I find that if I start talking about using drugs, my body will actually go through physical changes. My stomach will tighten up. I'll get butterflies. I may start sweating, or become anxious. I'll start to have cravings. In fact, scientific studies have shown that the presence of situations or people that have been previously associated with drug use can produce cravings and increase the risk of relapse. So it's important for me to avoid war stories that go into great detail about the times when I used to get high. If I find myself having one of these conversations, I'll end it right away, and call up a friend from the treatment center. It helps me reaffirm for myself why I'm in recovery, and how much better things really are now than they were when I was using.

Yes, I've said this before, but I can't emphasize enough the importance of asking for this kind of support during recovery. Calling a supportive friend is like being in a meeting, raising your hand, and saying, "This is what I'm feeling and this is what I'm going through. I need help processing these feelings in a healthy way." If you hold all that stuff in, you may make it for a while, but eventually those feelings and urges bottled up inside will consume you. I started and then continued using drugs not just because of physical addiction, but also because of the mountain of unresolved emotional conflicts and issues inside of me. Every time I started to come down from a high and got a glimpse of those issues, I ran as hard as I could to get away from them. I suppressed all those feelings, pushed all those bad memories away. Now I've learned to deal with them constructively, and one way to do that is to talk about them. You can talk about them in therapy, in a support group, or with a caring friend. The important point is to acknowledge your troubled feelings so that you can then work on healing them.

Just a Step Away...

There is no cure for addiction, and even when an addict has stayed clean for years or even decades, he or she is always just one step—a drink, a shot, a snort—away from starting again, sliding back down into chaos and despair. The changes that occur in the brain when one is addicted don't automatically correct themselves when using stops. The same cravings that used to drive me to hunt for heroin could be awakened again, and far more easily than in someone who was never addicted. That's why a major task of recovery is keeping those cravings from starting up. What's more, the decision to use drugs after a long period of abstinence is often an impulsive one—meaning that little rational thought goes into the decision. Teens have less impulse control than adults, so it's important for younger people to remember that, because their brains are still developing, they're particularly vulnerable to relapse.

> *The same cravings that used to drive me to hunt for heroin could be awakened again...*

I try to keep uppermost in my mind the idea that I need to be in charge of my actions—not some chemical. That means remembering what is important. For me, it's fulfilling my responsibilities to those who are counting on me. I have worked very hard to get free of drugs and to get started on the career that I have long hoped for. I am finally working at my chosen profession. At last, more than a decade after I did not succeed in becoming a Navy SEAL, I am a certified professional diver with a good job that can support my family and that I enjoy very much. I know that using drugs again would seriously jeopardize the good life I've managed to build for myself and my family, and I'll do whatever it takes to prevent that.

If a Relapse Occurs . . .

The possibility always exists that an addict in recovery will relapse. I know that this could happen to me, simply because it has happened to me so many times in the past. Relapses are simply a fact of recovery. But while they will occur from time to time, it's important to remember that they're not the end of the story. Some people will (understandably) panic after a relapse; they think they'll never be able to stay clean. That couldn't be more untrue. Just as you needed training wheels when you first learned to ride a bike, you need support and assistance when working on your recovery. Just because you fell off that bike a few (dozen) times doesn't mean you won't eventually learn how to ride it well. Ultimately, of course, it's important to work as hard as you can to prevent relapse, using strategies like the ones I've described in this chapter. But if or when a relapse does occur, your focus must shift to *containing* it, using the very same strategies:

Relapses are simply a fact of recovery.

- Continue with the type of therapy that helped you get clean in the first place.
- Avoid people and places that stimulate cravings—don't visit places where you once used, and avoid socializing

with people who still use drugs. End friendships with addicted friends.

- Stay busy and occupy yourself with non-drug activities.
- Get over your denial about your substance abuse problem.

Sometimes life hits you hard, and things happen that get you down. Those are the times when it can be hardest to maintain recovery, and those are the times when vigilance must be strongest and the techniques to stay clean applied most vigorously. Every addict in recovery needs skills training in avoiding and handling relapse. This is an important element of treatment, and it's one that everyone can master, whether literally following the strategies I've mentioned or adapting them in some way that suits that particular person. Bottom line: Do whatever you can to avoid returning to drug use. You can do it. I did.

Chapter Six

Looking Back, Looking Ahead

Y ou know the rest of my story (so far): a happy and loving wife, a daughter (and a step-daughter); a supportive and relieved family, and a good job. It's been incredibly hard work, earning back all the trust I threw away, all the while building a life for myself, working on maintaining my recovery, and staying clean. Every day is still a struggle, too, make no mistake. I'll bet you know that already, too.

Thinking back to how it felt to use drugs is something that I ordinarily try not to do, and I strongly recommend that you don't, either. It's a slippery slope back to substance abuse once you start reminiscing about the times you got high; when you find yourself doing that, take my advice and direct your thoughts elsewhere. And yet throughout the writing of this book, I wanted to at least look at that slope in order to convey to you the essence of what it is to be addicted to heroin, how I got hooked on it, what I did to break free, and most important, what I am doing now to try and stay free. If I knew some sacred utterance of warning about or release from the horrible bonds of addiction, I would tell you that, too. Surely had I known what it was myself, I would have been able to prevent oceans of pain—including my own.

My recovery is not perfect, nor will it probably ever be. Part of my job in life now is to critique my own behavior on a daily, sometimes minute-by-minute basis. I do not preach any particular brand of recovery, nor do I claim to have succeeded in finally slaying the dragon for good. I have, at one time or another, incorporated every possible means of self-correcting prescription— from twelve-step groups to methadone, from acupuncture to psychotherapy—into my quest for recovery. Some of those things worked better than others, but the one ingredient that has been there for me since I got sober and stayed that way was that commitment to staying clean. One thing I know for sure is that whether we have not used in one year or one day, we are still the same distance from the edge of madness. That distance is one shot of the drug, one puff, one sniff, one drink. The bottom line as I see it is to not use *at all costs.*

My recovery is not perfect, nor will it probably ever be.

"Real" Recovery Is Whatever Works for Us

Whatever it is that prevents an addict from picking up that next drink or taking that drug is as good as anything else, so if you've found something that works for you, hang on for dear life. Many recovering addicts will argue that this philosophy isn't to be considered *real* recovery. In their eyes that may be the truth, but as long as I do not have a needle in my arm and I can wake up every morning and appreciate the things I once took for granted, as long as I can wake up free from the life-draining habit that consumed me for over a decade, I can say that I have found at least some form of recovery.

Today, when I look at my baby daughter, I can see truth, beauty, and innocence. When my little step-daughter and I play in the park, I can see my own imagination and youth. When I lie awake next to my beautiful wife, listening to her quiet breathing, I can finally understand true love and trust—emotions that were once dead to me. This minute and the next and the one after that are what make up my life now. My recovery consists of knowing that for the sake of my family, my parents, and everyone who cares about and depends on me, and most of all, for my own sake, I can live *this minute* drug free.

Frequently Asked Questions

I know I need help; I just don't know how to get it.
Who do I ask? Who can I trust?

If you've recognized that you have a drug or alcohol abuse problem, good for you. Most young people don't seek help on their own; instead, they are referred to substance abuse treatment by the juvenile justice system, by a teacher or counselor at school, or by someone in their family. Being proactive about your problem and asking for help bode well for your recovery.

If you feel you can talk openly and honestly with your parents, they should be your first stop. Though they may react badly at first to the news that you've been using drugs, most parents want what's best for their kids. They should be able to locate a substance abuse expert in your area who specializes in adolescents.

Aside from your parents, you might talk to a school counselor, a trusted teacher, a member of your church, or your doctor. All of these individuals have access to information you can use in your efforts to get treatment. Just keep in mind that eventually your parents will probably have to be notified of the situation, so it might be best to go to them first.

For a list of organizations that can provide information on substance abuse treatment for young people, see the Resources section of this book.

How do I tell my parents?

Tell them the truth—that you need help, and that you trust them to get you the treatment you need. Don't be put off by their likely emotional reaction when you first tell them. They may be upset, but if you give them time, they'll mobilize their resources to help you in your recovery.

I drink on the weekends with my friends, and sometimes we smoke pot. But nothing bad has ever happened. Why should I stop?

Because eventually something bad will almost inevitably happen; whether it's something as immediate and serious as a bad car wreck, as seemingly minor as a fight with your boyfriend or girlfriend, or as remote as eventual damage to your body. Alcohol use by adolescents is responsible for increased accidents, assaults, and unprotected sex—not to mention that it's illegal, and you could run into trouble with the law if caught. Drugs may seem harmless now, but can have long-lasting effects upon your brain and the rest of your body. It's hard to believe that these invisible effects will eventually become harmful, but they will. Even smoking pot can cause long-term deficits in learning, thinking, and memory, and damage to the lungs. Furthermore, continuing to use drugs and alcohol now, as a teenager, vastly increases the likelihood that you'll develop a substance abuse problem as an adult.

Many of my family members have had drug and alcohol problems. Does that make me more likely to use drugs?

Researchers have concluded that young people who grow up with drug and alcohol use in the home are at higher risk for substance abuse themselves. This could be because they are influenced by witnessing family members using drugs; or it could be that they've inherited a genetic vulnerability to addiction that family members also have. The most likely scenario is that adolescents are at higher risk for *both* of these reasons. The good news is that just because drugs and alcohol were abused at home while you were growing up doesn't mean you will definitely use them yourself; just that the risk of doing so is higher. If you feel your own drug use may be related to that of family members, this is something to consider when seeking therapy. A psychotherapist may be able to help you work through some of these issues and recognize how to get past an unhealthy environment.

Why do I have to go into treatment? I can stop whenever I feel like it.

Ask yourself if that's really true, and if it is, then stop—for all of the reasons I've been discussing for over a hundred pages. The longer you continue to abuse drugs and alcohol, the more difficult it will be to stop when you decide to do so. If you find that you can't stop, then you have a sure sign that you have a substance abuse problem.

If you're still not convinced by all you've read so far, consider these words, written by a methamphetamine addict already in a drug rehabilitation program before completing college:

"How the hell did I get here? It doesn't seem that long ago that I was on the water-polo team. I was an editor of the school newspaper, acting in the spring play, obsessing about which girls I liked, talking Marx and Dostoevsky with my classmates. The kids in my class will be starting their junior year of college. This isn't so much sad as baffling. It all seemed so positive and harmless, until it wasn't." (Reprinted from David Sheff, "My Addicted Son," *New York Times Magazine,* February 2005.)

Drug use can get away from you very quickly; the safest course is to stop now, because if you wait until you have a full-blown addiction, recovery will be infinitely more difficult.

What is psychotherapy like? Will I have to lie on a couch and tell the doctor all about my mother?

These days, talking to a psychotherapist is a much more friendly and supportive experience than you might be envisioning from countless scenes on television and in the movies. If you end up in a session with a therapist, chances are that that person is experienced in working with people around your age, so he or she may understand your problems and the pressures and challenges you face better than you think. You may be encouraged to explore your feelings about your present situation, talk about substance abuse and the role it plays in your life, and examine past experiences and events that might have led you to use drugs. If the benefits of that still don't interest you, think of it as a nice big chunk of time where you're allowed to talk all about yourself. You may find you get more out of the experience than you expect.

I'm already getting treatment for my drug abuse, but I don't think it's helping. What should I do?

Talk to your counselor or therapist about your concerns. Honesty and forthrightness are key to making therapy work for you, and your therapists can't help you with a problem they don't know you're having. If, after discussing the issue with your treatment team, you decide that the program you're in isn't the one for you, you may be able to explore other options in your community. Your treatment team should be well qualified to help you locate another program or facility.

If, on the other hand, you've decided your treatment isn't helping because you're still experiencing cravings and urges to use drugs—but you haven't relapsed yet—give yourself some credit for resisting those cravings so far. Treatment won't be able to cure you of cravings, no matter how hard you work at it—not right away, at least. Cravings are a natural and unavoidable fact of life in recovery from addiction, and their presence does *not* indicate a failure on your part nor on the part of your treatment.

My friend told me alcoholism and drug addiction are diseases. What does that mean?

The diagnostic Bible of the mental health world, the *Diagnostic and Statistical Manual of Mental Disorders,* defines addiction as the physical abuse of, dependence on, and withdrawal from drugs and other miscellaneous substances. Addiction is thus classified as a mental illness, right along with such disorders as depression and schizophrenia. Once a drug user has advanced in his or her use of drugs to the point where tolerance develops and withdrawal symptoms occur if drug use stops, that person is said to have developed the brain disease of addiction. This means that addiction cannot be *cured* but must instead be *treated*, using all of the therapeutic and medical measures I've discussed in this book.

Should I tell everyone about my problems with drugs and alcohol?

This is a personal choice that each individual must make according to his or her own judgment. You certainly don't have to tell everyone you run into that you are in recovery from substance abuse, and doing so may very well provoke unwanted stigma and even discrimination.

On the other hand, it may be a good idea to disclose your status to close friends and family if they don't already know. The more people you have around to support you in your recovery, the better; their knowledge of your situation will also help prevent well-intentioned but problematic gestures such as invitations to bars, to go out clubbing, and so on. Also, if you are intimate with someone, it's my opinion that he or she has a right to know about your past.

Will my past troubles with substance abuse prevent me from having a job?

Discrimination against those recovering from substance abuse or addiction is against the law, but enforcement of such laws isn't always consistent. If you need not disclose your history to a potential employer, then don't; there's no point in revealing the information. If, on the other hand, a job application asks whether you've ever been convicted of a crime, and you have, you may find yourself forced to explain why. If you feel you have been discriminated against, there are advocacy organizations you can contact, such as the National Alliance on Mental

Illness (www.nami.org), or the Bazelon Center for Mental Health Law (www.bazelon.org).

What about starting a relationship with someone?

That's entirely up to you. I know that my wife has been incredibly supportive of me in my recovery; it would have been immeasurably harder without her help. A history of substance abuse can complicate relationships, but there's no reason yours should prevent you from dating and becoming involved with someone. Obviously I can't make any promises about your own relationship status, except to stress how dangerous it can be to your recovery should you become involved with someone who still uses drugs.

Glossary

addiction   A mental disorder characterized by the recurring compulsion to engage in some specific activity, such as drug or alcohol consumption, accompanied by tolerance and withdrawal symptoms if that activity ceases suddenly.

aftercare   Substance abuse follow-up treatment that occurs once a week or every two weeks, combined with urine screening and occasional individual counseling.

Alcoholics Anonymous (AA)   A nationwide support group of recovering alcoholics.

anxiety disorder   Any of several mental disorders that are characterized by extreme or maladaptive feelings of tension, fear, or worry.

attention-deficit hyperactivity disorder (ADHD)   A disorder characterized by a short attention span, excessive activity, or impulsive behavior. The symptoms of the disorder begin early in life.

barbiturate   A depressant used as a sedative.

behavior modification therapy   A form of therapy that focuses on changing or replacing unwanted behaviors.

benzodiazepine   A psychoactive drug that acts as a mild tranquilizer.

binge drinking   A single session of alcohol consumption that comprises five or more drinks for men and four or more drinks for women.

blood alcohol content (BAC)   The concentration of alcohol in the blood.

blood-brain barrier   A membrane-like structure that protects the brain from chemicals in the blood.

Buprenorphine   A medication prescribed to ease the symptoms of heroin withdrawal.

cannabis   The psychoactive product of the plant *cannabis sativa.*

cognitive-behavioral therapy   A form of psychotherapy that focuses on correcting inaccurate patterns of thinking and the behaviors that result from those patterns.

comorbidity   A co-occurring illness or disease.

conduct disorder   A disorder characterized by a repetitive or persistent pattern of having extreme difficulty following rules or conforming to social norms.

dependence   Physical reliance on a chemical substance such that tolerance develops and withdrawal symptoms appear if the substance is withdrawn suddenly.

depression   A disorder that involves being in a low mood nearly all the time, or losing interest or enjoyment in almost everything. These feelings last for at least two weeks and cause significant distress or problems in everyday life.

detoxification   The process of medically removing a chemical from one's body.

Diagnostic and Statistical Manual of Mental Disorders*, 4th Edition, Text Revision *(DSM-IV-TR)   A manual that mental health professionals use for diagnosing all kinds of mental illnesses.

dopamine   A neurotransmitter that is essential for movement and also influences motivation and perception of reality.

dual diagnosis   A situation in which one person is diagnosed with both a mental illness and chemical dependency.

eating disorder   A disorder characterized by serious disturbances in eating behavior.

electroencephalography   A technique that uses electrodes placed on the scalp to measure patterns of electrical activity emanating from the brain.

endorphins   Chemicals found within the brain that are associated with feelings of well-being.

euphoria   A state of very intense happiness and feelings of well-being.

euphoric recall   The process by which an addict remembers only the pleasurable feelings associated with drug use, and none of the negative ones.

family therapy   A form of talk therapy in which several members of a family participate in therapy sessions together.

glutamate   A stimulating neurotransmitter that promotes the flow of nerve signals in neurons.

group therapy   A form of talk therapy in which a group of people with similar problems work on specific issues together under the guidance of a therapist.

Hepatitis C   A severe viral infection of the liver, often contracted through the use of an infected hypodermic needle.

hippocampus   A brain structure involved in emotion, learning, and memory.

HIV/AIDS   A viral infection and its resulting immune system disease first reported in the United States in the 1980s, spread partially through the use of infected hypodermic needles and responsible for millions of deaths.

interpersonal therapy (IPT)   A form of psychotherapy that aims to address the interpersonal triggers for mental, emotional, or behavioral symptoms.

jaundice   A yellowing of the skin, eyes, and mucous membranes due to impaired liver function.

magnetic resonance imaging (MRI)   A powerful imaging technique that uses magnets and radio waves to produce pictures of body organs and tissues.

Medicaid A joint federal-state government program that provides health insurance to eligible low-income and disabled individuals.

mood disorder A mental disorder in which a disturbance of mood is the chief feature.

Naltrexone A drug used to manage alcohol and opioid dependence.

Narcan (Naloxone) A drug used to counter the effect of opioid or alcohol overdose.

Narcotics Anonymous (NA) A nationwide support group for recovering drug addicts.

neuron A nerve cell that is specially designed to send information to other nerve, muscle, or gland cells.

neurotransmitter A chemical that acts as a messenger within the brain.

obsessive-compulsive disorder (OCD) A mental disorder characterized by repeated, uncontrollable thoughts that cause anxiety as well as repetitive actions that the person feels driven to perform in response to these thoughts.

opiate A narcotic chemical found in opium.

opioid A chemical substance that has an opiate-like effect in the brain.

outpatient treatment A program of therapy, education, and relapse management for recovering substance abusers while they're living at home.

panic attack A sudden, unexpected wave of intense fear and apprehension that is accompanied by physical symptoms, such as a racing or pounding heart, shortness of breath, and sweating.

paranoia A disturbed thought process characterized by unreasonable anxiety, fear, and/or delusions of persecution.

positron emission tomography (PET) A medical imaging technique used to produce three-dimensional images or maps of areas in the human body.

post-acute withdrawal syndrome A group of symptoms of substance dependence that occur as the result of abstinence from addictive chemicals.

psychiatrist A medical doctor who specializes in the diagnosis and treatment of mental illnesses and emotional problems.

psychoactive substance A chemical that acts primarily on the central nervous system and alters brain function.

psychoeducational intervention A program of drug and addiction education for recovering substance abusers.

psychologist A mental health professional who provides assessment and treatment for mental and emotional disorders.

psychosis A symptom of severe mental illness characterized by delusions, hallucinations, and/or disordered thinking.

psychotherapy The treatment of a mental, behavioral, or emotional disorder through "talk therapy" and other psychological techniques.

receptor A molecule that recognizes a specific chemical, such as a neurotransmitter. For a chemical message to be sent from one nerve cell to another, the message must be delivered to a matching receptor on the surface of the receiving nerve cell.

relapse   A return of symptoms after a period of improvement.

residential treatment center   A treatment facility where the person lives in a dorm-like setting with a small group of people. The treatment is less specialized and intensive than in a hospital, but the stay may last considerably longer.

respiratory depression   An effect that occurs when ventilation is inadequate for the lungs to distribute oxygen to the body. Respiratory depression is a common result of heroin overdose.

reuptake   The process by which a neurotransmitter is absorbed back into the sending branch of the nerve cell that originally released it.

reward circuit   A group of sections and structures in the brain that work together to produce feelings of pleasure and satisfaction in response to certain stimuli.

risk factor   A situation, event, or circumstance that increases a person's likelihood of developing an illness.

schizoaffective disorder   A severe form of mental illness in which an episode of either depression or mania occurs at the same time as symptoms of schizophrenia.

schizophrenia   A severe, long-lasting mental disorder that produces symptoms such as distorted thoughts and perceptions, disorganized speech and behavior, and a reduced ability to feel emotions.

serotonin   A neurotransmitter that helps regulate mood, sleep, appetite, and sexual drive.

single photon emission computed tomography (SPECT)   An imaging technique that uses radioactive substances to create a two- or three-dimensional picture of the brain.

substance abuse   The continued use of alcohol or other drugs despite negative consequences, such as dangerous behavior while under the influence, or substance-related personal, social, or legal problems.

substance dependence   A state resulting from habitual use of drugs or alcohol, where tolerance has developed and withdrawal symptoms appear upon abstinence from the substance.

support group   A group that brings together people with a common concern so they can share support, encouragement, and hands-on advice.

synapse   The gap between two nerve cells that serves as the site where information is relayed from one cell to the next.

tetrahydrocannabinol (THC)   The main psychoactive substance found in marijuana and other forms of cannabis.

tolerance   The effect whereby a person's reaction to a drug decreases so that higher and higher doses are required to produce the desired effect.

twelve-step program   An addiction recovery plan developed and practiced by members of Alcoholics Anonymous, Narcotics Anonymous, and other mutual-help groups.

withdrawal   A set of symptoms that appear when a person abruptly ceases use of a psychoactive substance upon which he or she has become dependent.

Resources

Organizations

Substance Abuse or Mental Illness

American Academy of Child and Adolescent Psychiatry
3615 Wisconsin Ave. NW
Washington, DC 20016
(202) 966-7300
www.aacap.org
www.parentsmedguide.org

American Council for Drug Education
164 West 74th St.
New York, NY 10023
(800) 488-3784
www.acde.org

American Psychiatric Association
1000 Wilson Blvd., Suite 1825
Arlington, VA 22209
(888) 357-7924
www.psych.org
www.healthyminds.org
www.parentsmedguide.org

American Psychological Association
750 First St. NE
Washington, DC 20002
(800) 374-2721
www.apa.org
www.apahelpcenter.org
www.psychologymatters.org

National Alliance on Mental Illness
Colonial Place Three
2107 Wilson Blvd., Suite 300
Arlington, VA 22201
(800) 950-6264
www.nami.org

National Council on Alcoholism and Drug Dependence
244 East 58th St.
4th Floor
New York, NY 10022
(800) 622-2255
www.ncadd.org

National Institute on Alcohol Abuse and Alcoholism
5635 Fishers Ln., MSC 9304
Bethesda, MD 20892-9304
(301) 443–3860
www.niaaa.nih.gov
www.collegedrinkingprevention.gov

National Institute on Drug Abuse
National Institutes of Health
6001 Executive Blvd., Room 5213
Bethesda, MD 20892-9561
(301) 443-1124
www.drugabuse.gov
www.teens.drugabuse.gov

National Institute of Mental Health
6001 Executive Blvd., Room 8184, MSC 9663
Bethesda, MD 20892
(866) 615-6464
www.nimh.nih.gov

National Mental Health Association
2001 N. Beauregard St., 12th Floor
Alexandria, VA 22311
(800) 969-6642
www.nmha.org

National Mental Health Information Center
P.O. Box 42557
Washington, DC 20015
(800) 789-2647
www.mentalhealth.samhsa.gov

Substance Abuse and Mental Health Services Administration
1 Choke Cherry Rd.
Rockville, MD 20857
(800) 729-6686
www.samhsa.gov

Educational Issues

Office for Civil Rights
U.S. Department of Education
550 12th St. SW
Washington, DC 20202-1100
(800) 421-3481
www.ed.gov/ocr

Employment Issues

Americans With Disabilities Act
U.S. Department of Justice
Civil Rights Division, Disability Rights Section
950 Pennsylvania Ave. NW
Washington, DC 20530
(800) 514-0301
www.ada.gov

Legal Issues (General)

Bazelon Center for Mental Health Law
1101 15th St. NW, Suite 1212
Washington, DC 20005
(202) 467-5730
www.bazelon.org

Books

Anonymous. *Go Ask Alice*. New York: Simon and Schuster Children's Publishing, 1971.

Beckman, Chris. *Clean: A New Generation in Recovery Speaks Out*. Center City: Hazelden, 2005.

Gaughen, Shasta (Ed.). *Teen Addiction*. San Diego: Greenhaven Press, 2002.

Iverson, Leslie. *Drugs: A Very Short Introduction*. New York: Oxford University Press, 2001.

Knapp, Caroline. *Drinking: A Love Story*. New York: Dial Press, 1996.

Smith, Lynn Marie. *Rolling Away: My Agony with Ecstasy*. New York: Atria Books, 2005.

Teens Write Through It. Minneapolis: Fairview Press, 1998.

Volkman, Chris, and Toren Volkman. *From Binge to Blackout: A Mother and Son Struggle with Teen Drinking*. New York: New American Library, 2006.

Wurtzel, Elizabeth. *More, Now, Again: A Memoir of Addiction*. New York: Simon and Schuster, 2002.

Zailckas, Koren. *Smashed: Story of a Drunken Girlhood*. New York: Viking: 2005.

Websites

Al-anon/Alateen, (888) 4-AL-ANON, www.al-anon.alateen.org

Alcoholics Anonymous, (212) 870-3400 (check your phone book for a local number), www.aa.org

Cope Care Deal—A Mental Health Site for Teens, www.CopeCareDeal.org

Facts on Tap, Phoenix House, www.factsontap.org

Freevibe, National Youth Anti-Drug Media Campaign, www.freevibe.com

Narcotics Anonymous, (818) 773-9999, www.na.org

Partnership for a Drug-Free America, (212) 922-1560, www.drugfreeamerica.com

The New Science of Addiction: Genetics and the Brain, Genetic Science Learning Center at the University of Utah, www.gslc.genetics.utah.edu/units/addiction

Help for Related Problems

Anxiety Disorders

ORGANIZATIONS

Anxiety Disorders Association of America, (240) 485-1001, www.adaa.org

Freedom From Fear, (718) 351-1717, www.freedomfromfear.org

Obsessive-Compulsive Foundation, (203) 401-2070, www.ocfoundation.org

BOOKS

Ford, Emily, with Michael R. Liebowitz, M.D., and Linda Wasmer Andrews. *What You Must Think of Me: A Firsthand Account of One Teenager's Experience With Social Anxiety Disorder.* New York: Oxford University Press with the Annenberg Foundation Trust at Sunnylands and the Annenberg Public Policy Center at the University of Pennsylvania, 2007.

Kant, Jared Douglas, with Martin Franklin, Ph.D., and Linda Wasmer Andrews. *The Thought that Counts: A Firsthand Account of One Teenager's Experience with Obsessive-Compulsive Disorder.* New York: Oxford University Press with the Annenberg Foundation Trust at Sunnylands and the Annenberg Public Policy Center at the University of Pennsylvania, 2008.

Eating Disorders

ORGANIZATIONS

National Association of Anorexia Nervosa and Associated Disorders, (847) 831-3438, www.anad.org

National Eating Disorders Association, (206) 382-3587, www.nationaleating disorders.org

BOOK

Arnold, Carrie, with B. Timothy Walsh, M.D. *Next to Nothing: A Firsthand Account of One Teenager's Experience with an Eating Disorder.* New York: Oxford University Press with the Annenberg Foundation Trust at Sunnylands and the Annenberg Public Policy Center at the University of Pennsylvania, 2007.

Mood Disorders

ORGANIZATIONS

Child and Adolescent Bipolar Foundation, (847) 256-8525, www.cabf.org

Depression and Bipolar Support Alliance, (800) 826-3632, www.dbsalliance.org

Depression and Related Affective Disorders Association, (410) 583-2919, www.drada.org

Families for Depression Awareness, (781) 890-0220, www.familyaware.org

BOOKS

Irwin, Cait, with Dwight L. Evans and Linda Wasmer Andrews. *Monochrome Days: A Firsthand Account of One Teenager's Experience With Depression.* New York: Oxford University Press with the Annenberg Foundation Trust at Sunnylands and the Annenberg Public Policy Center at the University of Pennsylvania, 2007.

Jamieson, Patrick E., with Moira A. Rynn. *Mind Race: A Firsthand Account of One Teenager's Experience With Bipolar Disorder.* New York: Oxford University Press with the Annenberg Foundation Trust at Sunnylands and the Annenberg Public Policy Center at the University of Pennsylvania, 2006.

Suicidal Thoughts

ORGANIZATIONS

American Foundation for Suicide Prevention, (888) 333-2377, www.afsp.org
Jed Foundation, (212) 647-7544, www.jedfoundation.org
Suicide Awareness Voices of Education, (952) 946-7998, www.save.org
Suicide Prevention Action Network USA, (202) 449-3600, www.spanusa.org

BOOK

Lezine, DeQuincy A. and David Brent. *Eight Stories Up: An Adolescent Chooses Hope Over Suicide.* New York: Oxford University Press with the Annenberg Foundation Trust at Sunnylands and the Annenberg Public Policy Center at the University of Pennsylvania, forthcoming in 2008.

HOTLINES

National Hopeline Network, (800) 784-2433, www.hopeline.com
National Suicide Prevention Lifeline, (800) 273-8255,
    www.suicidepreventionlifeline.org

Schizophrenia

ORGANIZATIONS

National Schizophrenia Foundation, (800) 482-9534, www.nsfoundation.org
World Fellowship for Schizophrenia and Allied Disorders, (416) 961-2855, www.world-schizophrenia.org

BOOKS

Schiller, Lori, and Amanda Bennet. *The Quiet Room: A Journey Out of the Torment of Madness.* New York: Grand Central Publishing, 1996.
Snyder, Kurt, with Raquel E. Gur, M.D., Ph.D. *Me, Myself, and Them: A Firsthand Account of One Young Person's Experience With Schizophrenia.* New York: Oxford University Press with the Annenberg Foundation Trust at Sunnylands and the Annenberg Public Policy Center at the University of Pennsylvania, 2007.
Wagner, Pamela Spiro, and Carolyn S. Spiro. *Divided Minds: Twin Sisters and Their Journey Through Schizophrenia.* New York: St. Martin's Press, 2005.

Bibliography

American Psychiatric Association. *Diagnostic and Statistical Manual of Mental Disorders* (4th ed., text revision). Washington, DC: American Psychiatric Association, 2000.

Colman, Andrew. *Oxford Dictionary of Psychology.* New York: Oxford University Press, 2001.

Drugs, brains, and behavior: The science of addiction. National Institute on Drug Abuse. http://www.drugabuse.gov/scienceofaddiction/. Accessed 8/6/07.

Ehlers, Cindy. Neurobehavioral consequences of adolescent nicotine exposure. Tobacco-Related Disease Research Program Grant Page. http://www.trdrp.org/fundedresearch/Views/Grant_Page.asp?grant_id=1942. Accessed 8/6/07.

Evans, Dwight L., and Linda Wasmer Andrews. *If Your Adolescent Has Depression or Bipolar Disorder: An Essential Resource for Parents.* New York: Oxford University Press with the Annenberg Foundation Trust at Sunnylands and the Annenberg Public Policy Center at the University of Pennsylvania, 2005.

Evans, Dwight L., Edna B. Foa, Raquel E. Gur, Herbert Hendin, Charles P. O'Brien, Martin E. P. Seligman, and B. Timothy Walsh (Eds.). *Treating and Preventing Adolescent Mental Health Disorders: What We Know and What We Don't Know.* New York: Oxford University Press with the Annenberg Foundation Trust at Sunnylands and the Annenberg Public Policy Center of the University of Pennsylvania, 2005.

Foa, Edna B., and Linda Wasmer Andrews. *If Your Adolescent Has an Anxiety Disorder: An Essential Resource for Parents.* New York: Oxford University Press with the Annenberg Foundation Trust at Sunnylands and the Annenberg Public Policy Center at the University of Pennsylvania, 2006.

Gaughen, Shasta (Ed.). *Teen Addiction.* San Diego: Greenhaven Press, Inc., 2002.

Goldstein, Avram. *Addiction: From Biology to Drug Policy* (2nd Ed.). New York: Oxford University Press, 2001.

Gur, Raquel E., and Ann Braden Johnson. *If Your Adolescent Has Schizophrenia: An Essential Resource for Parents.* New York: Oxford University Press with the Annenberg Foundation Trust at Sunnylands and the Annenberg Public Policy Center at the University of Pennsylvania, 2006.

Iversen, Leslie. *Drugs: A Very Short Introduction.* New York: Oxford University Press, 2001.

Leshner, Alan. Treating the brain in drug abuse. *NIDA Notes* 15:4 (2000).

Mathias, Robert. NIDA pursues many approaches to reversing methamphetamine's neurotoxic effects. *NIDA Notes* 15:4 (2000).

McCrady, Barbara, and Elizabeth Epstein. *Addictions: A Comprehensive Guidebook.* New York: Oxford University Press, 1999.

NIAAA Interdisciplinary Team on Underage Drinking Research. Developmental issues in underage drinking research. *Alcohol Research & Health* 28:3, (2004/5): 121–123.

Parks, George, and Alan Marlatt. Relapse prevention therapy: A cognitive-behavioral approach. *The National Psychologist* 9:5 (2000).

Prescription drugs: Abuse and addiction. *NIDA Research Report Series,* NIH Publication Number 05–4881, August 2005.

Ramage, S.N. et al. Hyperphosphorylated tau and amyloid precursor protein deposition is increased in the brains of young drug users. *Neuropathol Appl Neurobiol* 31:4 (2005): 439–48.

Robson, Philip. *Forbidden Drugs* (2nd Ed.). New York: Oxford University Press, 1999.

Schiller, Lori, and Amanda Bennet. *The Quiet Room: A Journey Out of the Torment of Madness.* New York: Grand Central Publishing, 1996.

Sheff, David. My addicted son. *NY Times Magazine,* February 6, 2005.

Smith, Lynn Marie. *Rolling Away: My Agony with Ecstasy.* New York: Atria Books, 2005.

Teens Write Through It. Minneapolis: Fairview Press, 1998.

Tobacco control and teens. American Lung Association. http://www.lungusa.org/site/pp.asp?c=dvLUK900E&b=22940. Accessed 8/6/07.

Vogel, Julie, et al. The relationship between depression and smoking in adolescents. *Adolescence* 38:149 (2003): 57–74.

White, A., and Swartzwelder, H. Age-related effects of alcohol on memory and memory-related brain function in adolescents and adults. *Recent Dev Alcohol* 17 (2005): 161–176.

Zailckas, Koren. *Smashed: Story of a Drunken Girlhood.* New York: Viking, 2005.

Index

AA. *See* Alcoholics Anonymous
Acamprosate, 117*t*
Acid. *See* LSD
Addiction
  comorbid disorders and, 38–43,
    89–90, 93, 118–21, 129
  definition of, 9, 32–33
  disease categorization of, 11–12,
    145–46
  dosage/administration of drugs and,
    66–67
  escapism through, 56–57
  manipulation aspect of, 22–23, 48
  physical symptoms of, 11
  psychological symptoms of, 11, 32
  substance abuse v., 8–9, 26
  tolerance's relation to, 10–11, 32,
    67–69, 74, 81, 87, 88, 145.
    See also Alcohol; Drug(s);
    Progression of addiction; Substance
    abuse
ADHD. *See* Attention-deficit
  hyperactivity disorder
Adolescent Mental Health Initiative
  (AMHI), ix, xi
  web sites associated with, x
Adolescents
  ADHD and, 43
  alcohol use by, 27–29, 31, 73–75

anxiety disorder statistics on, 40
brain chemistry/structure of, 35
cigarette smoking by, 77, 84, 89–90
cocaine use by, 84
conduct disorders and, 43
drug/substance use statistics on, 28–30,
  73
eating disorders and, 42
heroin use by, 30
inhalant use by, 85
marijuana use by, 28, 76, 88
mood disorder statistics on, 39
prescription drug use by, 87, 88
research geared towards, 44
resources, support, for, x, 107*t*, 156,
  157, 158
risk factors, substance abuse, for, 3–4,
  27–30, 33
treatment tailored towards, 101–2,
  114–16
Adoption studies, 36
Aerobic exercise, 127
Aftercare, treatment, 103, 114, 129
Age-related risk factors, 35–36
AIDS, 47, 82, 107
  needle exchange programs and,
    82*t*
Al-Anon, 107*t*, 156
Alateen, 107*t*, 156

Alcohol, 12
    adolescent use of, 27–29, 31, 73–75
    binge drinking and, 75*t*
    brain's reaction to, 66, 74
    case study focus on, 9–10*t*, 17–20, 31
    diagnosis of abuse of, 73–74
    diagnosis of dependence on, 74
    eating disorders and use of, 42
    gender considerations related to, 75,
        75*t*
    marketing of, 28–29
    ramifications, physical, of, 9, 10*t*, 71,
        73, 74, 75*t*
    ramifications, psychological, of, 9, 73,
        74, 75*t*
    tolerance development and, 10–11,
        74
    withdrawal from, 34–35, 74, 104.
        See also Addiction; Substance abuse
Alcoholics Anonymous (AA), 105, 130*t*,
        156
    recovery maintenance through,
        129–30
    twelve steps in, 106–7*t*
Alzheimer's disease, 70
Amphetamines, 83, 84
Angel dust. *See* Phencyclidine
Annenberg Foundation Trust at
        Sunnylands, ix
Anorexia nervosa, 42
Antabuse. *See* Disulfiram
Antipsychotic medication, 42*t*
Anxiety, 93
    drug use symptom of, 25
    eating disorder symptom of, 42
Anxiety disorders, x
    addiction's co-occurrence with, 40
    medications for, 131
    occurrence statistics on, 40
    panic attacks and, 93
    resources, support, for, 156–57
    types of, 40
Assessment, substance abuse, 102–4
Attention-deficit hyperactivity disorder
        (ADHD), 43
Availability, substance, 38, 44, 125–28,
        136

Barbiturates. *See* Depressants
Bazelon Center for Mental Health Law,
        147, 155–56
Behavior modification treatment, 96,
        108
Benzodiazepines, 87–88, 93
    withdrawal from, 104
Binge drinking, 75*t*
Biological factors, addiction, 34
    brain chemistry variances and, 35.
        See also Brain
Bipolar disorder, x
    addiction's co-occurrence with, 39–40,
        129
    characteristics of, 39
Black tar heroin (Mexican Mud), 55, 56
Book resources, mental health support,
        156, 157, 158
Brain
    adolescent structure of, 35
    blood-brain barrier and, 60, 81
    chemical copycats and, 64–66, 79, 80,
        81, 84
    damage, 12–13, 59–60, 70–72, 72*t*, 77,
        84, 85, 86
    neurotransmitters and receptors in,
        62–66, 68, 69, 79, 80, 81, 84
    reaction to substances within, 34–35,
        59–72, 74, 76–90
    reward system within, 61–62, 63–70,
        81, 84
    tests related to, 70–71, 72*t*
    tolerance development by, 10–11, 32,
        67–69, 74, 81, 87, 88, 145
Bulimia nervosa, 42
Buprenorphine (Suboxone), 104, 116,
        117*t*, 122

Cannabis sativa, 76–78. *See also* Marijuana
Case study, author
    alcohol use in, 17–20, 31
    arrests in, 51–52, 58, 94–95, 96–97
    career aspirations in, 21, 23–24, 97–98
    childhood/family background in,
        15–17, 18, 27
    cocaine use in, 5–6, 24–25
    depression highlighted in, 24–25

detox highlighted in, 48–51, 52, 54, 58,
    92, 101
escapism in, 56–57
halfway houses in, 54, 92, 101
heroin use in, 3–6, 25–27, 30–33,
    46–59, 91–92, 94–101
homelessness in, 4–6, 54, 55, 56–58
LSD use in, 21–23
marijuana use in, 20–21, 22, 31
methamphetamine use in, 23–24
overdose in, 93–94
OxyContin use in, 93–94
recovery highlighted in, 122–24,
    138–39
rehab highlighted in, 58, 92, 97, 101
relapse in, 49–51, 53–54, 58–59,
    91–101, 124
self-esteem highlighted in, 7–8, 16–17,
    18–19, 22, 25
suicidal thoughts in, xiii, 56
withdrawal highlighted in, 5–6, 46–47,
    56, 58, 95
CBT. See Cognitive-behavioral therapy
Cigarettes. See Smoking, tobacco
Club drugs, 85
    types of, 86
    withdrawal from, 86, 87
Cocaine, 12
    addiction rate related to, 84
    brain's reaction to, 84
    case studies on use of, 5–6, 24–25,
        41–42t
    "cotton fever" reaction to, 5–6
    crack-, 67, 83–84
    eating disorders and use of, 42
    forms of, 83
    ramifications, physical, of, 83, 84
    ramifications, psychological, of, 84
    schizoaffective disorder and,
        41–42t
    withdrawal from, 25, 83
Codeine, 80–81
    brain's reaction to, 65
    prescription, 87
    withdrawal from, 34, 69
Cognitive-behavioral therapy (CBT),
    108

Comorbid disorders, 38–43, 89–90, 93
    substance abuse treatment and,
        118–21, 129. See also Related mental
        health disorders
Conduct disorder, 43
Cost, treatment, 113, 118
    government assistance with, 120t
    insurance and, 120t
    sliding scales for, 121t
"Cotton fever," 5–6
Crack-cocaine (free base), 67, 83–84
Cravings management, 135
    activity-planning and, 125–27, 137
    continuous support/treatment for,
        129–31, 136
    temptation avoidance for, 126, 127–28,
        136
Critique of Pure Reason (Kant), 19

Date rape. See Sexual assaults
Delirium tremens (DT), 74
Denial, 137, 143–44
Depp, Johnny, 26
Depressants, 87–88, 93, 104
Depression, x, 145
    addiction's co-occurrence with, 11, 33,
        39–40, 89, 93, 129
    case study highlighting, 24–25
    characteristics of, 39
    eating disorder symptom of, 42
    occurrence statistics on, 39
Detoxification (detox), 102
    aftercare and, 50
    case study highlighting, 48–51, 52, 54,
        58, 92, 101
    characteristics of, 104–5
    rewards of, 50
Dextroamphetamines, 83, 88
Diagnostic and Statistical Manual of
    Mental Disorders (DSM-IV), 73, 74,
    145
Disulfiram (Antabuse), 117t
Doctors. See Medical practitioners
The Doors (band), 19
Dopamine, 66, 80, 86, 88
    cocaine and, 84
    hallucinogens and, 78

Drug(s)
  brain chemistry/reaction to, 34–35, 59–72, 74, 76–90
  club, 85–87
  depressants, 87–88, 93, 104
  dosages of, 66–67
  Ecstasy, 31t, 86
  experimentation with, 27–30
  hallucinogens, 21–23, 78–79
  inhalants, 84–85
  Lithium, 21
  long-term effects of, 70–72
  LSD, 21–23, 78–79
  marijuana, 9–10t, 20–21, 22, 28, 31, 42, 65, 67, 71, 76–78, 84, 88, 142
  opiates, xiii, 3–6, 12, 25–27, 30–33, 34, 46–59, 65–67, 69–70, 80–82, 87, 91–101
  Percocet, 21
  prescription, 87–88
  Seconal, 21
  stimulants, 5–6, 12, 23–25, 41–42t, 42, 67, 70–71, 83–84, 87, 88
  tolerance, 10–11, 32, 67–69, 81, 87, 88, 145
  Valium, 21, 87–88
  Vicodin, 21. *See also* Addiction; Alcohol; Brain; Medications, treatment; Substance abuse; *specific drugs*
Drug testing, 97, 99, 105
DSM-IV. See Diagnostic and Statistical Manual of Mental Disorders
DT. *See* Delirium tremens

Eating disorders, x
  addiction's co-occurrence with, 42
  resources for support of, 157
  types of, 42
Ecstasy (MDMA), 31t
  brain's reaction to, 86
Educational interventions, 112
EEG. *See* Electroencephalography
Electroencephalography (EEG), 71
Employment. *See* Work
Encephalins, 65
Endorphins, 65

Environment
  extracurricular activities in, 38, 125–27, 137
  risk factors related to, 15–17, 27–30, 36, 37–38, 44, 143. *See also* Family; Friends/peers; Relationships, romantic
Euphoric recall, 133–34
Evans, Dwight L., ix
Exercise, 127

Family
  addiction risks related to, 27, 36–38, 143
  detox expectations and, 50–51
  disclosure to, 146
  enabling by, 55
  rebuilding bonds with, 111, 131–32
  support by, 111–12, 127, 141–42
  therapy, 111–12
Flashbacks, 79
Foa, Edna B., ix
Free base. *See* Crack-cocaine
Freon, 85
Frequently asked questions
  on danger of substance use, 142
  on denial of problem, 143–44
  on disclosure of addiction, 142, 146–47
  on disease categorization, 145–46
  on employment/work, 146–47
  on relationships, 147
  on risk factors, 143
  on therapy, 144
  on treatment, 141–42, 145
Friends/peers
  disclosure to, 146
  rebuilding trust of, 131–32
  support by, 111, 127, 134–35
  temptation avoidance and, 126, 127–28, 136

Gammahydroxybutyrate (GHB), 86–87
Gender
  alcohol consumption and, 75, 75t
  prescription drug use and, 88
  risk factors associated with, 37–38
  treatment related to, 103, 116

Generalized anxiety disorder, 40
Genetic risk factors, 36–37, 143
GHB. *See* Gammahydroxybutyrate
Government assistance, 120*t*
Group therapy, 111
Gur, Raquel E., ix

Halfway houses, 54, 92, 101
Hallucinogens
    LSD, 21–23, 78–79
    mescaline, 78
    peyote, 78
    psilocybin mushrooms, 78
Hendin, Herbert, ix
Hepatitis C, 47, 58, 82
    needle exchange programs and, 82*t*
Heroin, 12
    addiction statistics for, 30, 81
    black tar, 55, 56
    brain's reaction to, 65, 66, 81
    case study on use of, 3–6, 25–27,
        30–33, 46–59, 91–92, 94–101
    dosage/administration of, 47, 66–67,
        81
    "hillbilly," 93
    ramifications, physical, of, 32–33, 58,
        66–67, 70, 81–82
    ramifications, psychological, of, xiii,
        5–6, 32–33, 56, 58–59, 91, 94–95,
        98–99
    tolerance development and, 32, 81
    withdrawal from, 5–6, 32–33, 34,
        46–47, 56, 58, 69, 82, 95
"Hillbilly heroin." *See* OxyContin
HIV. *See* Human Immunodeficiency
    Virus
Home groups, 92
Homelessness, 4–6, 54, 55, 56–58
Human Immunodeficiency Virus (HIV),
    47, 82, 107
    needle exchange programs and, 82*t*

Individual counseling. *See* Psychotherapy
Inhalants, 84, 85
Insurance, 120*t*
Intensive outpatient treatment, 102,
    112–13

Internet resources, x, 82, 118, 156
Interpersonal therapy (IPT), 109
IPT. *See* Interpersonal therapy

K. *See* Ketamine
Kant, Immanuel, 19
Kat valium. *See* Ketamine
Ketamine, 79, 86
    sexual assaults and, 80
Kierkegaard, Soren, 7, 19

Leary, Timothy, 21
Legal issue resources, 155–56
Lifestyle
    continuous support and, 129–31,
        133–35, 136
    daily focus on recovery and, 13,
        133–35, 138, 139
    healthy activities and, 125–27, 137
    modification strategies and, 112
    temptation and, 126, 127–28, 136
Lithium, 21
LSD (acid)
    brain's reaction to, 78–79
    case study on use of, 21–23
    forms of, 78

Magnetic resonance imaging (MRI), 70, 71
Manipulation, 22–23, 48
Marijuana, 84
    administration of, 67, 76
    adolescent use of, 28, 76, 88
    brain's reaction to, 65, 76–77
    case studies on use of, 9–10*t*, 20–21,
        22, 31
    eating disorders and use of, 42
    ramifications, physical, of, 71, 77, 142
    schizophrenia triggered by, 42
    suicidal thoughts related to, 77
    withdrawal from, 78
MDMA. *See* Ecstasy
Medicaid, 120*t*
Medical practitioners, x, 103, 107–14, 110*t*
Medications, treatment
    acamprosate, 117*t*
    antipsychotic, 42*t*
    anxiety disorder, 131

Medications (*continued*)
  buprenorphine, 104, 116, 117*t*, 122
  disulfiram, 117*t*
  methadone as, 52, 93, 95, 104, 117*t*
  mood disorder, 131
  naltrexone, 117*t*
  Narcan, 94
  stimulant, 43
Meditation, 126–27
Melthylphenidate (Ritalin), 88
Mental health professionals, x, 103,
    107–14, 110*t*
Mephobarbital, 87–88
Mescaline, 78
Methadone
  addiction treatment using, 52, 93, 95,
    104, 117*t*
  street, 52
Methamphetamine, 12, 83
  crystal, 23–24
  ramifications of use of, 70–71, 84
Mexican Mud. *See* Black tar heroin
Monitoring the Future study, 28
Mood disorders
  addiction's co-occurrence with, 39–40,
    89, 93
  bipolar, x, 39–40, 129
  depression, x, 11, 24–25, 33, 39–40,
    42, 89, 93, 129, 145
  medications for, 131
  resources for support of, 157–58
Morphine, 65, 80–81
  prescription, 87
Morrison, Jim, 19–20
MRI. *See* Magnetic resonance imaging

NA. *See* Narcotics Anonymous
Naltrexone, 117*t*
Narcan, 94
Narcotics Anonymous (NA), 106–7*t*, 123,
    129–30, 156
  outpatient treatment and, 105
National Alliance on Mental Illness,
    146–47, 154
National Highway Traffic Safety
    Administration, 77

National Institute on Alcohol Abuse
    and Alcoholism (NIAAA), 73,
    154
Navy, 21, 23–24, 98
Needle exchange programs, 82*t*
Neurons, 66, 68, 84, 86
  function of, 62–64
Neurotransmitters
  chemical copycats and, 64–66, 79, 80,
    81, 84
  function of, 62–64
  tolerance buildup and, 68
  withdrawal's influence on, 69
NIAAA. *See* National Institute on
    Alcohol Abuse and Alcoholism
Nicotine, 67
  brain's reaction to, 66
  schizophrenia and, 41. *See also*
    Smoking, tobacco
Nietzsche, Friedrich, 19
Norepinephrine, 78, 86
Novocaine, 83

O'Brien, Charles P., ix
Obsessive-compulsive disorder, 40
Opiates
  brain's natural, 65
  codeine, 34, 65, 69, 80–81, 87
  damage, physical, caused by, 32–33, 58,
    66–67, 70, 81–82
  heroin, xiii, 3–6, 12, 25–27, 30–33, 34,
    46–59, 65–67, 69–70, 80–82,
    91–92, 93, 94–101
  morphine, 65, 80–81, 87
  opium, 80–81
  oxycodone, 80–81, 87
  OxyContin, 87, 93–94
  prescription, 87
  withdrawal from, 5–6, 32–33, 34,
    46–47, 56, 58, 69, 82, 87, 95.
    See also specific opiates
Opioids, 65, 69, 87
Opium, 80–81
Organizational resources
  for job discrimination, 146–47
  for related disorders, ix–x, 157, 158

for substance/mental abuse, 73, 118,
    153–55
for support meetings, 106–7*t*
Outpatient treatment
    characteristics of, 105–7, 111, 112
    intensive, 102, 112–13
Overdose, 93–94
Oxycodone, 80–81, 87
OxyContin ("hillbilly heroin"), 87, 93–94

Panic attacks, 93
Paranoia, 11, 25
Parkinson's disease, 71
PCP. *See* Phencyclidine *(PCP)*
Percocet, 21
PET. *See* Positron emission tomography
Peyote, 78
Phencyclidine (PCP), 22, 79
    brain's reaction to, 80
Positron emission tomography (PET), 70,
    71
Post-acute withdrawal syndrome, 122–23
Post-traumatic stress disorder (PTSD), 40
Prescription drugs
    commonly abused, 87
    gendered use of, 88
Progression of addiction
    addiction phase in, 32–33
    brain stages in, 10–11
    case studies reflecting, 9–10*t*, 12,
        17–27, 30–33, 31*t*, 46–59, 91–101
    experimentation phase in, 30–31
    hazardous use phase of, 32
Psilocybin mushrooms, 78
Psychiatric illness. *See* Addiction; Related
    mental health disorders
Psychoeducational interventions, 112
Psychotherapy (talk therapy)
    behavioral, 108
    CBT, 108
    counseling v., 109–10
    doctors/practitioners of, 103, 107–14,
        110*t*
    effectiveness of, 145
    family, 111–12
    frequently asked questions on, 144–45

group, 111
IPT, 108–9
recovery maintenance via, 129–31
PTSD. *See* Post-traumatic stress disorder

The Quiet Room (Schiller), 41–42*t*

Reagan, Nancy, 12
Receptors, protein (brain)
    chemical copycats and, 64–66, 79, 80,
        81
    function of, 63–64
    tolerance buildup and, 68
Recovery, xiv, xv–xvi, 3, 12
    activities recommended aiding, 126–27
    case study highlighting, 122–24,
        138–39
    commitment's relation to, 99–101, 139
    craving management in, 125–31, 135,
        136–37
    daily focus on, 13, 133–35, 138, 139
    family's role in, 111–12, 127, 141–42
    friends' role in, 111, 127, 134–35
    rebuilding trust during, 131–32
    reentry into society in, 131
    rewards of, 7, 14
    self-esteem building in, 132–33.
        See also Treatment, substance
        abuse
Rehabilitation (rehab), 58, 92, 97, 101
Relapse
    avoidance, 112, 135–36, 139
    case study on, 49–51, 53–54, 58–59,
        91–101, 124
    containment of, 136–37
    euphoric recall leading to, 133–34
    prevention therapy for, 112
Related mental health disorders
    addiction's co-occurrence with, 38–43,
        89–90, 93, 118–21, 129
    ADHD, 43
    anxiety disorders, x, 40, 93, 131,
        156–57
    cigarette use and, 41, 77, 84, 89–90
    conduct disorder, 43
    eating disorders, x, 42, 157

Related mental health disorders
    (*continued*)
    mood disorders, x, 11, 24–25, 33,
        39–40, 42, 89, 93, 129, 131, 145,
        157–58
    schizoaffective disorder, 41–42*t*
    schizophrenia, x, 40–42, 145, 158.
        See also specific disorders
Relationships, romantic, 146, 147. *See also*
    Friends/peers
Religion, 38
Resources, support
    for adolescents, x, 107*t*, 156, 157,
        158
    for anxiety disorder, x, 156–57
    book, 156, 157, 158
    for eating disorders, 157
    education-related, 155
    employment-related, 146–47, 155
    for financial matters, 120–21*t*
    Internet, x, 82, 118, 156
    for legal issues, 155–56
    for locating treatment, 118
    for medical community, x
    for mood disorders, 157–58
    organizational, ix–x, 73, 106–7*t*, 118,
        146–47, 153–55, 157, 158
    for schizophrenia, 158
    for substance abuse/mental illness, ix–x,
        73, 82, 106–7*t*, 118, 146–47,
        153–55, 156
    for suicidal thoughts, 158
    for support meetings, 106–7*t*
Respiratory depression, 66, 81, 87
Risk factors, 13, 45
    age-related, 35–36
    availability of substance and, 38, 44
    biological, 34–35
    environmental/social, 15–17, 27–30,
        36, 37–38, 44, 143
    genetic, 36–37, 143
    mental health disorder-related,
        38–43
    teenagers and, 3–4, 27–30, 33
    trauma/abuse/neglect as, 44
Ritalin. *See* Melthylphenidate
Rolling Away (Smith), 31*t*, 72*t*, 156

SAMHSA. *See* Substance Abuse and
    Mental Health Services
    Administration
Schiller, Lori, 41–42*t*
Schizoaffective disorder, 41–42*t*
Schizophrenia, x, 145
    addiction's co-occurrence with,
        40–42
    drugs as triggers of, 42
    resources for support of, 158
Schopenhauer, Arthur, 19
Seconal, 21
Self-esteem
    building acceptance and, 132–33
    case study on issues of, 7–8, 16–17,
        18–19, 22, 25
Seligman, Martin E. P., ix
Serotonin, 78, 79, 84, 86
Sexual assaults
    alcohol and, 73, 75*t*
    GHB and, 87
    ketamine and, 80
Single photon emission
    computed tomography (SPECT),
        71
Smashed (Zailckas), 130*t*, 156
Smith, Lynn Marie, 31*t*, 72*t*
Smoking, tobacco, 41
    adolescent, 77, 84, 89–90
    ramifications of, 89. *See also*
        Nicotine
Social anxiety disorder, 40
Special k. *See* Ketamine
SPECT. *See* Single photon emission
    computed tomography
Speedballs, 5
Stimulants
    amphetamine, 83, 84
    cocaine, 5–6, 12, 24–25, 41–42*t*, 42,
        67, 83–84
    dextroamphetamine, 83, 88
    melthylphenidate, 88
    methamphetamine, 12, 23–24, 70–71,
        83, 84
    prescription, 87. *See also specific
        stimulants*
Suboxone. *See* Buprenorphine

Substance abuse
definition of, 8–9
ramifications, physical, of, 12–13, 58,
59–62, 70–72, 72t, 76–77, 81–82,
84, 85, 86, 87, 88, 89
ramifications, psychological, of, xiii,
5–6, 9, 13, 32–33, 56, 58–59, 73,
74, 75t, 77, 79, 84, 88, 89–90,
91, 94–95, 98–99
resources, support, for, ix–x, 82,
106–7t, 118, 146–47, 153–55,
156
substance dependence v., 8–9. *See also*
Addiction; Alcohol; Drug(s)
Substance Abuse and Mental Health
Services Administration (SAMHSA),
118, 155
Substance dependence. *See* Addiction
Suicidal thoughts
depression's relation to, 39
drug use's association to, xiii, 56, 77
resources, support, for, 158
Synapses, brain, 62–63, 66, 84

TCH. *See* Tetrahydrocannabinol
Teenagers. *See* Adolescents
Teens Write Through It, 10t, 156
Temptation avoidance, 126, 127–28,
136
Tetrahydrocannabinol (TCH), 65,
76–77
Therapeutic community treatment,
95–96, 101, 122
Therapy. *See* Psychotherapy
3,4-methylenedioxy-methamphetamine.
See Ecstasy
Tolerance
alcohol, 10–11, 74
drug, 10–11, 32, 67–69, 81, 87, 88,
145
*Treating and Preventing Adolescent Mental
Health Disorders* (AMHI), x
Treatment, substance abuse
acceptance of disorder and, xiv, 137,
143–44
adolescent-specific, 101–2, 114–16
aftercare in, 103, 114, 129

behavior modification in, 96
commitment's relation to, 99–101
comorbid disorder treatment and,
118–21
costs of, 113, 118, 120–21t
detox, 48–51, 52, 54, 58, 92, 101, 102,
104–5
educational interventions in, 112
family therapy in, 111–12
gender considerations in, 103, 116
group therapy in, 111
halfway houses in, 54, 92, 101
home groups in, 92
individual counseling in, 107–10,
110t
medications used in, 43, 52, 93, 94, 95,
104, 116, 117t
options, locating of, for, 118
outpatient, 102, 105–7, 111–13
personalization of, xv, 101–2, 103,
114–18, 139–40
progression/length of, 91, 129–31
referral and assessment in, 102–4
rehab, 58, 92, 97, 101
relapse in, 49–51, 53–54, 58–59,
91–101, 112, 124, 133–34, 135–37,
139
residential, 103, 113–14
therapeutic community, 95–96, 101,
122
21 Jump Street (television show), 19, 26

Valium, 21, 87–88
Vicodin, 21
Vitamin K. *See* Ketamine

Walsh, B. Timothy, ix
Withdrawal
alcohol, 34–35, 74, 104
case study highlighting, 5–6, 46–47,
56, 58, 95
cocaine, 25, 83
codeine, 34, 69
depressants and, 88, 104
DT during, 74
ecstasy, 86
GHB, 87

Withdrawal (*continued*)
  heroin, 5–6, 32–33, 34, 46–47, 56, 58,
    69, 82, 95
  marijuana, 78
  medical supervision of, 69, 88, 104
  opiate, 5–6, 32–33, 34, 46–47, 56, 58,
    69, 82, 87, 95
  physical effects of, 11, 32–33, 34–35,
    46–47, 69, 74, 78, 82, 83, 86–87
  post-acute syndrome related to, 122–23
  psychological effects of, 11, 25, 33, 58,
    69, 74, 78, 82, 83, 86–87

Work
  addiction's impact on, 47–48, 146–47
  career aspirations and, 21, 23–24,
    97–98
Writing, 126
www.CopeCareDeal.org, x
www. nasenorg, 82
www.oup.com/us/teenmentalhealth, x

Xanax, 87–88, 93

Zailckas, Koren, 130*t*